A Community of Self-Reliance

The New Consensus on Family and Welfare

Michael Novak	Lawrence Mead
John Cogan	Donald Moran
Blanche Bernstein	Charles Murray
Douglas J. Besharov	Richard P. Nathan
Barbara Blum	Richard J. Neuhaus
Allan Carlson	Franklin D. Raines
Michael Horowitz	Robert D. Reischauer
S. Anna Kondratas	Alice M. Rivlin
Leslie Lenkowsky	Stanford Ross
Glenn C. Loury	Michael Stern

American Enterprise Institute for Public Policy Research
Washington, D.C.

Marquette University
Milwaukee, Wisconsin

The members of the Working Seminar are grateful to the Lynde and Harry Bradley Foundation and the John M. Olin Foundation for their very generous financial support; to the American Enterprise Institute for administrative assistance and the use of its facilities during many working sessions; and to the Charles Stewart Mott Foundation for additional financial support during the final phases of the Seminar's work.

Distributed by arrangement with

UPA, Inc.
4720 Boston Way
Lanham, MD 20706
3 Henrietta Street
London WC2E 8LU England

ISBN 0-8447-3623-6

ISBN 0-8447-3624-4 (pbk.)

AEI Studies 456

Printed in the United States of America

Contents

A Note about
the Working Seminar

The Working Seminar on Family and American Welfare Policy is composed of scholars and practitioners from several institutions, many backgrounds, and a broad range of points of view. Several recent administrations are represented, as are scholars from several major research institutions and universities. Michael Novak is the chairman and John Cogan the vice chairman of the Working Seminar.

The Working Seminar is sponsored by the Institute for Family Studies of Marquette University, whose director is Jay Gubrium. The members of the Working Seminar are grateful to the Lynde and Harry Bradley Foundation and the John M. Olin Foundation for their very generous financial support; to the American Enterprise Institute for administrative assistance and the use of its facilities during many productive working sessions; and to the Charles Stewart Mott Foundation for additional financial support during the final phases of the Seminar's work.

As groundwork for this report, the Working Seminar commissioned a dozen major research papers, which will appear in print during 1987. The titles and authors of the commissioned papers are listed in the appendix.

The Members of
the Working Seminar

MICHAEL NOVAK (Chairman): George Frederick Jewett Scholar in Religion and Public Policy; director, Social and Political Studies, the American Enterprise Institute

JOHN COGAN (Vice Chairman): Principal associate director, Hoover Institution; former associate director for human resources, Office of Management and Budget; former assistant secretary for policy, U.S. Department of Labor; author of several articles on negative income taxation and black teen-age employment

BLANCHE BERNSTEIN: Consultant on social welfare policy; former commissioner, New York City Human Resources Administration; author of *Saving a Generation* and numerous other studies

DOUGLAS J. BESHAROV: Resident scholar, American Enterprise Institute; former director, U.S. National Center on Child Abuse and Neglect

BARBARA BLUM: President, Foundation for Child Development; past president, American Public Welfare Association; former commissioner, New York State Department of Social Services

ALLAN CARLSON: President, Rockford Institute; author of numerous essays on the family, welfare, and culture

MICHAEL HOROWITZ: Partner, Dickstein, Shapiro & Morin; former counsel to director of the Office of Management and Budget

S. ANNA KONDRATAS: Former Schultz Fellow for Health and Urban Affairs, Heritage Foundation;* co-author, *Beyond Welfarism* (forthcoming)

LESLIE LENKOWSKY: President, Institute for Educational Affairs; author of *Politics, Economics, and Welfare Reform* and numerous essays on welfare reform

GLENN C. LOURY: Professor of political economy, Kennedy School of Government, Harvard University; author of *Free at Last? Racial Advocacy in the Post–Civil Rights Era* (forthcoming)

---

*Served on the Seminar until her recent appointment as Director, Office of Analysis and Evaluation, U.S. Department of Agriculture.

LAWRENCE MEAD: Associate professor of politics, New York University; author of *Beyond Entitlement* and other studies of work requirements and other obligations in social policy

DONALD MORAN: Vice president, ICF Incorporated; former executive associate director, Office of Management and Budget

CHARLES MURRAY: Fellow, Manhattan Institute; author of *Losing Ground: American Social Policy 1950–1980*

RICHARD P. NATHAN: Professor of public and international affairs, Woodrow Wilson School, Princeton University; chairman, Manpower Demonstration Research Corporation

RICHARD J. NEUHAUS: Director, Center on Religion and Society; author of *To Empower People* and other works on mediating structures

FRANKLIN D. RAINES: General partner, Lazard Freres & Co.; former member, White House Domestic Policy staff

ROBERT D. REISCHAUER: Senior fellow, Brookings Institution; former deputy director, Congressional Budget Office

ALICE M. RIVLIN: Director, Economic Studies, the Brookings Institution; former director, Congressional Budget Office

STANFORD ROSS: Partner, Arnold and Porter; former commissioner, Social Security Administration

MICHAEL STERN: Vice president, R. Duffy Wall & Associates; former staff director, Senate Finance Committee

Staff

DOUGLAS J. BESHAROV, administrator
KATHLEEN MCINNIS, coordinator
KARL ZINSMEISTER, research director
SCOTT WALTER, research assistant
JUDY SHINDEL, administrative assistant
LYNDA MCAVOY, administrative assistant
PRISCILLA M. GALLERANO, administrative assistant
GAYLE YIOTIS, manuscript typist

Introduction

A good society is judged by how well it cares for its most vulnerable members.

No person should be involuntarily poor without others coming to his or her assistance.

No able adult should be allowed voluntarily to take from the common good without also contributing to it.

Low income and behavioral dependency are two quite different problems and require different remedies.

A New Public Consensus

Profoundly moved by the growing crisis in family and welfare, many concerned observers have struggled to build consensus on *what to do*. The crisis itself is plain enough. Consider these few developments:

- Since 1965, the fastest growing segment of the poor (now 30 percent of all the poor) has been single mothers and their children under eighteen.
- Children in poverty are now 3.7 times more numerous than the elderly poor.
- Almost half (46 percent) of children on Aid to Families with Dependent Children (AFDC) in 1983 were born to parents not joined in marriage.
- 270,000 teen-agers had children out of wedlock in 1983; 229,000 had children in wedlock; and another 450,000 had abortions.
- Among poor blacks concentrated in high-poverty tracts in the central cities of the nation's hundred largest metropolitan areas, single-parent families have come to outnumber married-couple families by more than three to one, and illegitimacy rates in some poverty tracts have surpassed 80 percent.

The current chairman of the Senate Subcommittee on Social Security and Family Policy, Senator Moynihan, recently quoted from a prominent demographer: in recent years, "an earthquake shuddered through the American family structure."[1] As the elderly and others have been lifted above the government poverty line, female-headed families have been falling below it—and often for reasons having to do with their own social behavior. For such reasons, both Democrats and Republicans, the White House and the Congress, and students of poverty from all points on the political spectrum are re-examining the bases of American family life.

Along with other factors, this change in family structure now underlies the new face of poverty in America. Unless something is done about it, poverty will persist in certain sectors even despite economic growth; and if economic growth fails, a massive disaster impends. Worst-case poverty is now largely (but not entirely) an urban phenomenon and is considerably more concentrated than in

1970 in the nation's hundred, fifty—or even twenty—largest cities. It is no longer characterized solely by low income (indeed, those involved in drug trafficking, prostitution, or other off-the-books activities do not invariably suffer from low income) but also by self-damaging social behaviors, especially with regard to family life.

This portion of the poverty population is not large, compared with the total numbers of the poor. But its poverty appears to be different in kind. Its ranks appear to be swelling. And its internal sufferings are particularly acute. What makes the picture saddest of all is that so much of its dependency upon the public purse appears to be rooted in personal behaviors—a matter which is not easy for public policy to address. Nonetheless, the sharp distinction between these two types of dependency—objective dependency upon the public purse and behavioral dependency—is an important key to sound public policy for reducing poverty in the years ahead.

Because this distinction has not always been taken into account, some observers have come to see existing welfare policy as toxic; they believe that it is damaging the very poor it intends to help. Even if welfare policy has not *caused* the widespread behavioral dependency that has now become so highly visible, at the very least existing public policies have done little to remedy the situation.

Nonetheless, faced with the human suffering implicit in the current condition of so many of today's poor, there has come to be something like a new consensus concerning new directions. "Conservatives" have come to see that the nation must do something about the increasing numbers of vulnerable ones, women and children chiefly, but also the males who in more normal times would have stood side-by-side with females as breadwinners for their offspring. "Liberals" have come to see that welfare programs should have an ethical component, a signaling function, and that behavioral dependency must be addressed. Movement from right and left has established new common ground, just as the nation is summoning its strength to tackle anew the unfinished business of family and welfare.

Our Working Seminar has cooperated over many months in remarkable amity, civility, much agreement, and courteous disagreement. We have proceeded by way of consensus, drawing upon the quite diverse experiences and convictions of our members. Since we represent a broad spectrum of philosophies, the degree of consensus we have achieved may seem surprising. We ourselves were not certain until the end that it could be done.

We all, however, had the same factual situation to confront and from the outset recognized that each of our different viewpoints contained some measure of the truth and that serious persons of goodwill can narrow their disagreements without surrendering their basic divergences. Besides, since unintended consequences and painful irony nearly always flow from even the best designed public policies, some humility goes with the territory. We hope the consensus we have been able to reach is a good omen for the country.

If the country puts its mind to it, we believe, there are a multitude of things we could be doing that we are not doing, that would help many to begin contributing their fair share to the common life. Not least of these is to change our ways of seeing the problem and to change the *ethos* surrounding family, work, and neighborhood.

Some twenty years after the War on Poverty declared by President Lyndon B. Johnson, there is hope for a new era of social inventiveness. Much has been learned; there have been serious disappointments; there have also been successes. The record shows that the generation of Americans since 1962 has been extremely generous and has allocated privately and through state and federal government hundreds of billions of dollars to help the poor. They do not mind spending money, but they do want to see results. Surely, Americans think, a nation spending as much as we do each year on social welfare payments can do better than we are now doing. There *must* be better ways. The trick is to find them.

The Working Seminar's inquiries have led us to at least four points of new emphasis: first, to focus on the difficult problems of behavioral dependency and inability to cope; second, to call vivid attention to children and the family; third, to stress the social obligations inherent in welfare benefits; and, fourth, to call upon all major institutions of American society, not only government, to change the way in which they address the poor.

Since the problems of poverty concern the whole people, including voluntary as well as governmental institutions, we direct this report to all our fellow citizens, rather than to the small circle of public policy experts and poverty scholars. While at times we must use the language of social science, we do our best to make the present situation clear in plain English.

The first aim of our Working Seminar has been to use modes of analysis that come as close to daily human reality as possible. We have tried to present not just accurate numbers, but also many other human dimensions—often not easily quantifiable—of the condition of the poor.

Second, the test we propose for ourselves and for the country is whether, ten or twenty years from now, the condition of the needy and the vulnerable in our society will have been significantly improved.

But there was also a third goal: not to miss a historic opportunity. The Reagan administration announced early in 1986 that it would undertake a new beginning in welfare policy, particularly with respect to the family. Since both "conservatives" and "liberals" now wish to attack these recalcitrant problems afresh, a new consensus affords an opportunity that should not be missed.

Our method of proceeding is straightforward. In part one, we set forth seven components of the starting place many observers have now come to share. These seven "starting places" form a philosophical underpinning for social policy during the coming years. They are echoed in our recommendations.

In part two, we describe the current situation as accurately as the data and our common interpretations permit. We try to discover what the dependency that concerns us actually *is*. We explore its several manifestations and puzzle over its hidden dimensions.

In part three, we set forth recommendations touching on the full array of institutions in our society, voluntary and governmental, from local to national levels. All of us have responsibilities regarding the most vulnerable of our fellow citizens.

We are especially concerned for the children of the behaviorally dependent. The very young represent the future of the republic; a wise society cannot ignore them. In the crucial early years of life, the family is the main incubator of the habits of free citizens; hence, the family is at the center of our study.

As Tocqueville pointed out, without a populace practicing the habits requisite to their support, free institutions cannot stand. Liberty dwells first in the habits a people acquire in the home and develop throughout the institutions, large and small, of society as a whole. Thus, American society is a commonwealth of a special sort, dependent upon the exercise of responsibilities by each and every citizen. It is a society that demands much of individuals, because it expects them to be free. The source of the nation's beauty, and of the love its citizens bear it, is that it asks so much of them.

One main contribution of the Working Seminar is to make serious demands both upon the behaviorally dependent, because it sees in them fellow citizens, and upon every major institution in American society, not government alone.

Note

1. Daniel Patrick Moynihan, "Beyond Welfare," Statement before the Senate Subcommittee on Social Security and Family Policy, January 23, 1987 (mimeo), p. 5. The demographer quoted was Samuel Preston.

PART ONE
Starting Places of the New Consensus

A few weeks back many of us who watch television news came upon the term "syzygy," by which astronomers describe a rare alignment of the sun, the moon and the earth which causes all manner of natural wonders. We may just have one of those rare alignments that bring about genuine social change.

SENATOR DANIEL PATRICK MOYNIHAN
January 1987

This is the time to reform this outmoded social dinosaur and finally break the poverty trap.

PRESIDENT RONALD REAGAN
January 1987

1

A Community of Self-Reliance

In some countries, the inhabitants . . . set too high a value upon their time to spend it on the interests of the community; and they shut themselves up in a narrow selfishness, marked out by four sunk fences and a quickset hedge. But if an American were condemned to confine his activity to his own affairs, he would feel an immense void in the life which he is accustomed to lead, and his wretchedness would be unbearable.

ALEXIS DE TOCQUEVILLE

Free Persons in Cooperation

From the beginning, Americans have prided themselves on the power of their institutions to provide opportunities by which the poor regularly escape from poverty. "Send me your tired, your poor," the Statue of Liberty says. In the long history of our country, millions of individuals and families of all races and backgrounds have begun in poverty and during their lifetime climbed out of it. This process continues before our eyes.

The people of the United States have always cherished two traits, cooperation and self-reliance. Empowered by both traits, our forebears founded new communities. They experimented with and established new institutions. Together our forebears put up one another's barns, built churches and schools, constructed civic buildings, and freely undertook common tasks. Each family cherished its own independence; each was equally glad to lend a hand to a neighbor.

These two traits, self-reliance and community, serve us in good stead as we face contemporary problems of poverty and dependency. Americans want to help each other out. But they also expect one another to be self-reliant. Every right, they recognize, involves reciprocal duties. Each citizen should contribute to the common good, as well as benefit by it. The Americans most admired by other Americans acquit their responsibilities to self and to others—are both cooperative and self-reliant.

3

For this reason, signs of poverty and dependency deeply trouble the American conscience. It is not only our people's compassion that is touched. They also sense that, if dependency grows, and if this dependency is especially acute in certain communities, something is *wrong* (not just economically wrong but morally wrong), affronts the whole meaning of the American experiment, and needs to be set right.

The free society must by its very nature regard each citizen as responsible, self-reliant, and self-governing. Each citizen is trusted to be pursuing that self-mastery which lies at the heart of "the pursuit of happiness." Only citizens able to govern themselves can fulfill the social duties inherent in a self-governing republic. Out of such a sense of self, every citizen bears many obligations and duties to others and to the polity.

Yet freedom also means, alas, the freedom to fail. The "creative destruction" characteristic of a dynamic system means that at every point in time some citizens are experiencing failure. In addition, a system built to human proportions includes personal fallibility, too. Thus, its own love of liberty presents a free and just society with intricate problems.

Today, for example, significant numbers of American adults are not demonstrating the behaviors expected of free and responsible citizens. Linked to poverty among an important fraction of the poor is a high incidence of dropping out from school, of failure to prepare themselves for future employment, of begetting children out of wedlock, of crime, of drug use, and of other visible disorders. Such persons—whose numbers appear to be growing—are the behaviorally dependent, since their need for help from others springs in significant measure from their own behaviors. Since many persons who begin in such environments triumph over them, hope remains. The puzzle is, Why do others fall into such disorders and remain trapped in them?

For such failures, no believer in the personal responsibilities of the free citizen should wholly shift responsibility from the individual to the environment. To do so would mean denying the responsible humanity of those who falter and the noble achievement of those who, overcoming formidable obstacles, do not. Honoring those who succeed, we try to find ways of opening new opportunities for those left behind.

Thus, we have tried to ask: What are the causes of the *successful* habits of citizens? We examine how these may be undergirded by institutional supports. Unless one knows clearly how to increase the incidence of successful behaviors, concentration upon the dysfunctional may breed discouragement.

4

It is not entirely a mystery how many climb from poverty. Some specific behaviors empower them. The probabilities of remaining involuntarily in poverty are remarkably low for those who

- complete high school
- once an adult, get married and stay married (even if not on the first try)
- stay employed, even if at a wage and under conditions below their ultimate aims

Those who do these three traditional things may experience periods in poverty but are quite unlikely to stay involuntarily poor.[1] By no means foolproof, these are the methods that have worked, and are still working, for millions.

In 1987, a substantial minority of the poor is suffering from something more than the low income familiar in family memory to most Americans. This new thing, which we have called "behavioral dependency," is more like an inability to cope. Many of the poor need order in their surroundings and in their lives; they need the intellectual and moral skills that enable them to escape from poverty and to live as full and independent citizens. Low income is comparatively easy to remedy; to overcome behavioral dependency requires a much more human, complex, and difficult engagement.

What can our private and public institutions do better, so as to decrease the incidence of behavioral dependency?

Where can individuals who wish to escape from such disorders turn for help?

Without claiming to have come to the bottom of these difficult questions, we have reached agreement upon seven starting places crucial to their solution.

New (and Old) Starting Places

Economic growth is necessary but not sufficient. Although the new consensus recognizes that economic growth alone is not sufficient to overcome dependency, still, among the necessary preconditions for that task, nothing is a greater driving force. Alice M. Rivlin has written:

> In a growing economy public choices are less agonizing and divisive. It is possible to modernize the armed forces; keep the nation's infrastructure in repair; provide for the elderly, the sick, and the needy; improve education and other public services; and still have private incomes that rise after taxes. Public choices are never easy, but they generate far more

5

our perception of Poverty

conflict in a declining or stagnating economy, when an increase in the resources to meet one kind of need requires an absolute reduction of resources used to meet other needs.[2]

Economic growth generates jobs and new opportunities. It generates revenues that make government poverty programs possible. It facilitates the generosity of the fortunate and rewards the efforts of the needy. It is particularly important for democracies, since only economic growth allows all to hope that through their own well-designed projects and efforts each can better his condition. Economic growth encourages individuals to compare their present condition with their expected future condition, rather than with the condition of others. Economic growth encourages all to work cooperatively; with it, democracy can depend upon generosity of spirit. By contrast, a stagnant or declining economy breeds envy and discord.

But economic growth also has two other aspects. Through the inventions and discoveries that make it happen, economic growth steadily transforms the conditions of daily life—not least, among the poor. In addition, the economic growth of the past has shaped, often unconsciously, the way in which Americans think of poverty.

Since the beginnings of our republic, economic growth has steadily transformed the lives of succeeding generations. It has entailed more than an increase in the quantity of goods and services; it has meant a transformation in the kinds of goods and services available. No wealthy gentleman of two hundred years ago ever took the wheel of a Ford pickup. None could see a doctor with hope that the influenza of a beloved child could be cured; that an inflamed liver could be treated; that a broken leg could be X-rayed. (Doctors bled George Washington to death.) The teeth of the wealthy were likely to be brown, rotten, and broken. Their homes, too, lacked indoor heating, plumbing, electric light, a telephone, a radio, television, a toaster, a dishwasher, a washer-dryer. Even in 1940, four out of ten American homes lacked indoor plumbing.[3]

What we mean by poverty, therefore, changes because of the diffusion of technologies that often go unremarked in writings on poverty. Consider recent dramatic improvements in the health of the poor. In the United States, such improvements, while speeding up for the population as a whole after 1960, have been most consequential for disadvantaged groups. During the decade from 1973 to 1983, when income measures began showing greater poverty, life expectancy at birth increased by more than three years for all, but even more sharply for poorer groups. Even while the governmental poverty rate for children under eighteen was rising by a third, the infant

6

mortality rate fell by about one-third. Almost across the board, advances were made by groups at higher risk of poverty than by others. Life expectancy at birth rose 3.0 years for whites, but 5.2 years for nonwhites.[4] For American Indians in or around tribal territories, the infant mortality rate in 1955 was more than twice as high as the national average; by 1982, it measured lower than the nation's average.[5]

Second, our very notion of poverty contains within it an expectation of economic growth. Not long ago poverty meant living just above subsistence. By now it means a level of basic decency, and this level is expected to rise slowly with the times. Thus, our goals for diminishing poverty have come to include de facto six components. All presuppose the broad diffusion of new inventions and new technologies, not only in medicine but also in the instruments of daily living. These six components are:

• Decade by decade, the proportions of the poor ought to be reduced.

• Decade by decade, the standard of expectable necessities required for a decent standard of living should rise. This includes such mundane measures as household appliances and living space, but also such important measures as higher standards of longevity, of infant mortality, and of health.

• Every able-bodied poor person ought to have the opportunity to exit from poverty. If the poverty of some is persistent, or if it persists among particular groups over long periods, something seems seriously wrong.

• Those of the poor unable to exit from poverty, through no fault of their own but because of disability, illness, or old age, should find adequate assistance from others, including government as a last resort.

• Those of the poor who can through their own efforts exit from poverty should be able to find the jobs necessary for them to do so.

• Given an open society and personal effort, talent should often emerge (and be rewarded) among persons born poor; and their invention, creativity, and personal liberty should flourish. Thus, the free circulation of individuals in both upward and downward mobility should respond primarily to individual talent, effort, and opportunity.

All six of these components of the nation's working notion of poverty rest upon our experience of economic growth and the sense of sustained progress it engenders in us. Because we have experienced economic growth, we are optimistic about reducing poverty.

7

Looked at from the other side, neither stagnation nor recession are good for the poor. High inflation devastates the poor, especially those on fixed incomes. Persistent high unemployment is bad for the poor. All failures to maintain economic growth hurt the poor more than others. That is why the new consensus emphasizes that programs designed to help the poor must be consistent with economic growth. This is true even though economic growth alone is not sufficient, since those habituated to dependency or ill-prepared for self-reliance often do not take advantage of it.

A second necessary step is to "disaggregate" the poor, that is, to sort out the kinds of poverty. Persons of low income are not an undifferentiated mass; they are as complex in their situations, circumstances, motivations, and sense of well-being as any other part of the population. Perhaps, all things considered, they are even more so.

Clearly, the needs of poor persons over sixty-five are not identical to those of poor youngsters under six. The needs of a single person are not identical to those of a couple with young children. An adequate income for a family of four in Hibbing, Minnesota, is not likely to provide a similar family in the South Bronx with equivalent standards of schooling, diet, basic health, living quarters, and physical safety. Again, an early-retired civil servant with accumulated possessions who owns a mortgage-free rural retreat, while reporting an annual income that would place him below the government's poverty line, is likely to enjoy a far higher standard of living than younger neighbors with a growing family whose dollar income is equal to his.

From the standpoint of public policy, disaggregation is crucial. Programs successful in helping one sort of poor person may harm (or bypass) another. And some households may not present a problem for public policy simply by virtue of having a monetary income defined as poor.

We shall discuss the varieties of poverty in more detail in part two. But even at this point it may be worthwhile to use a first rough sketch presented recently by Mary Jo Bane, executive deputy commissioner of New York State's Department of Social Services.

- Between 35 and 40 percent of the nation's poor in the mid-1980s were children and their caretakers in families headed by women . . . this group has grown substantially as a proportion of the poor over the last 15 years.

- About a fifth of the nation's poor are either elderly or so disabled that they cannot work enough to support their families.

- Only about 6 percent of the poor in 1980 were blacks or Hispanics living in those areas of the 100 largest cities of the country that were 40 percent or more poor . . . . In New York state, by contrast, that number is 20 percent of the poor in inner-city ghettos, still a minority, but large enough to give New Yorkers a somewhat different perspective on the problem.[6]

A certain humane care is necessary, therefore, in describing the poor and in specifying which of many types of poverty is intended. Some persons are a danger to their own best interests; their behaviors are patently self-damaging. Others, through no fault of their own, are down on their luck. Still others, though in poverty, are taking steps that will soon lead to their exit from it. Some endure passively; others follow the ways of ambition, perhaps without success, perhaps with thankful good fortune. Thinking about poverty demands close attention to *personal realities*. Generalizations need to be tested against daily experience. Well-intended rules, formulated from afar, may have ironic, even tragic, effects.

The battle against poverty is a long one; in recent years, we have seen new successes for some, deterioration in the conditions of others. The American habit of trying to make one another feel guilty can sometimes undermine the common high morale necessary to continue steadfastly in common projects. Instead of taking comfort from gains made, while girding themselves for greater efforts, Americans are sometimes bombarded with "evidence" that all their efforts are for nought. Far from inspiring greater efforts, such approaches sap the public's patience. An effort to reduce poverty is not a twenty-year task; it is never ending. It must go on steadily, constantly relying on and appealing to the capacity of free persons to make successful choices. For that reason, it is important for the public to know of progress achieved.

Between 1965 and 1985, the meaning of poverty, as officially measured, has changed substantially. By official measures, the proportions of Americans living in poverty have not fallen dramatically. In 1965, 17 percent of Americans were below the official line; in 1973, the figure was 11 percent; in 1985, 14 percent.[7] Nonetheless, the official poverty line defines a less insecure position today than formerly, because of many new noncash government benefits. The availability of Medicare in 1985, disbursing $65 billion to 20 million patients, has helped to change the meaning of poverty for the elderly.[8] Food stamps and other sorts of aid available today, but not in 1965, help the impecunious to attain a far more secure material level than twenty years ago.

Indeed, it is not only those *in* poverty whose material situation has been improved, but those kept *out of* poverty as well. In 1985, using the broadest official measure, there were over 7 million families

9

not below the poverty line because of government aid in all forms, including social security payments, cash assistance, and noncash benefits such as food stamps and housing supplements.[9]

Monetarily, in 1985, about 1 million of the nation's 7 million poor families fell short of the poverty line by less than $1,000; and another million by less than $2,000. Assuming that cash transfers had no disincentive effects on the earnings or behavior of recipients, one could bring all the poor over the poverty line with about $48 billion.[10] For many years actual antipoverty spending has been far in excess of that figure. Such calculations illustrate that merely supplying cash is not enough to solve the problems that most worry the nation regarding poverty, most notably the problem of behavioral dependency.

Finally, it is worth noting that means-tested noncash benefits given to the poor and the near-poor in 1985 totaled $56 billion. This compares with $5.9 billion in 1965 (in 1985 dollars).[11] Two different perspectives here come into play. If that $56 billion were simply divided among 7 million poor families, it would amount to an average of nearly $8,000 each year per family. This has led some to argue simply for "cashing out" all benefits for the poor, in order to eliminate poverty (as an income shortfall) by a redefinition of benefits as income for the poor. But that method, though mechanically simple, would not suffice for those among the poor who may need forms of aid that go far beyond income supplements, such as instruction, counseling, and employment. In some environments, even an income above the poverty line would leave many in a wretched condition.

In 1966, 29 percent of those over sixty-five were below the government's poverty line; by 1985, this number had fallen to 13 percent —and to as little as 3 percent if noncash benefits, notably Medicare, are included.[12]

On the other side of the ledger, improvements in the lot of the elderly since 1965 have been fatefully matched by growing numbers of children suffering from the spread of behavioral dependency. The number of children below the official poverty line is now 3.7 times the number of the elderly poor: 13.0 million vs. 3.5 million.[13] Before reaching the age of eighteen, one out of every three American children is now likely to spend at least some years in a poverty household.[14] In 1983 a fifth of all American births, and nearly three-fifths of all births to black Americans, were illegitimate.[15]

As we look toward the end of the century, it is helpful to seek comfort in progress made since 1965, as a ground for further advances.

Money alone will not cure poverty; internalized values are also needed.

Money income alone does not define poverty. The connotations of the word poverty today suggest something beyond low income, just as its opposite, "living well," is not adequately defined by income measures, but is in part a matter of values realized and personal orderliness attained. The word reflects both an objective, official assessment and a subjective, personal assessment. Thus, a family of newly arrived Asian immigrants with an annual income well below the official poverty line may not think of itself as poor. It may have every confidence that with skill and hard work, of the sort to which it has been accustomed and in which it finds significant satisfaction, it will not for long linger in poverty. Meanwhile another family on the same street, even with a higher annual income, may be far less spirited, determined, or socially organized.

Obviously the economy does fail some people for a time, as when the only plant in a local community closes down, or where an entire city whose main economic base is linked to a faltering industry experiences massive unemployment. Nonetheless the most disturbing element among a fraction of the contemporary poor is an inability to seize opportunity even when it is available and while others around them are seizing it. Some may have work skills in the normal sense, but find it difficult to be regular, prompt, and in a sustained way attentive to their work. Their need is less for job training than for meaning and order in their lives. Those involved in job training have been obliged to teach basic personal habits and attitudes as much as vocational skills.

The most visible of the nation's poor—those approximately 5 million citizens in poverty areas in the hundred largest metropolitan areas, the so-called underclass (to be considered more fully in part two)—have especially forced this theme upon researchers and observers. The name underclass has entered the language both because a condition worse than low income alone has arisen and because this condition seems to violate American traditions of upward mobility. Many of its component factors appertain more to internal morale and personal control than to income alone. Public neutrality with respect to its manifest behavior and attitudes would represent complicity. In such circumstances, compassion demands a moral response from public policy: an insistence upon the same public standards as well as opportunities for all.

Thus, a penumbra of hidden meanings distorts many discussions of poverty. A seemingly objective measure of monetary income is employed. But the problems of some of the poor would not be solved by an income above the poverty line alone, and others of the officially defined poor do not really present a public policy problem—they are taking care of themselves.

Consider the poor who own their own homes, maintain their families in high morale, eagerly acquire skills making them employable, learn to read and to express themselves, are active in their communities, and participate in civic projects. Such persons, even though poor, properly have high self-esteem, and seem also by others to be performing admirably. They may well have economic needs—tuition assistance for the education of their children, help for a special medical problem, or higher-paying employment. Still, their competence and habits have them poised to benefit by economic growth and by better employment opportunities. The challenges posed for public policy by such forms of poverty are straightforward and relatively easy to meet.

By contrast, those who do not manifest such competences are needy in more fundamental ways. For the latter, neither economic growth nor opportunities for employment are sufficient. This part of the poverty population has need of a far more penetrating compassion, directed at achieving control over their lives, the ability to cope, readiness for employment, and the like. Such persons can scarcely be helped by income supplements alone. The help they need runs deeper and requires significant person-to-person involvement.

At this level, assistance to the poor becomes a humanistic task. To take the full needs of the vulnerable seriously is not "blaming the victim." Like others the poor know that self-respect is crucial to personal fulfillment and that self-respect is hard earned. In the words of the old maxim: Better than giving a man a fish is to teach him how to fish.

Moreover, most American families came to America poor, many within living family memory, and across the generations many have also experienced significant upward and downward income mobility. Even in their individual lives, many have experienced episodes of poverty or fears thereof, since the ups and downs of income usually follow the normal patterns of age—low at first, higher, then down again—and many of life's events add other complex patterns. Thus, those public policies and privately organized institutions that extend support to those in temporary need are the sinews of the republic: extending relief, charity, a scholarship, a job, a loan, a subsidy, an interview—a break. All human beings are needy creatures; most fortunate are those for whom need becomes opportunity.

In short, the many varieties of poverty require researchers to go beyond questions of low income, in order to attend to questions concerning the way persons organize their lives. It is not enough for the makers of public policy to attend to externalities and public

12

arrangements, without also being aware of the ways in which policy impinges—or fails to impinge—on questions of personal and social values. Escape from poverty is in part a matter of attaining personal control and independence, so as to respond to changing circumstance.

An indispensable resource in the war against poverty is a sense of personal responsibility. A free country depends heavily on a sense of responsibility among its citizens. In addition, since the benefits of society in some ways are in fact received by all, all correspondingly have responsibilities to the common good. On the personal side of the ledger, a sense of responsibility is essential to self-respect and to a fulfilling life. On society's side, it is essential to the good of the whole. For both reasons, it would be wrong to think of persons without attributing to them a sense of duty and responsibility.

The nation values self-reliance; both the good of individuals and the common good depend on it. Often in the past, programs designed to help persons of low income have offered benefits but without imposing any social obligations in return. This is to treat such persons as less than full citizens. It is to ignore their bonds and obligations to the public. To hold all persons responsible, to the extent of their abilities, for acquiring those skills and competences necessary to self-reliance is only just. To hold those on welfare personally responsible for finding self-sustaining employment is no more than is asked of other citizens. To be sure, some large fraction of such persons is in need of assistance in order to prepare themselves for exercising the full responsibilities of citizens. Such help should be given, but in such a way that they may fulfill their own share of social obligations.[16]

A significant proportion of those who fall into poverty today do so through changes in family status: divorce, separation, or having a child out of wedlock. These are clearly matters of personal responsibility. The largest and fastest-growing segment of the poverty population consists of women and children affected by such events, who in increasing numbers fall back upon the public purse. In this way, the fact that several million young men and women do not provide for their families has become a public concern.

The national ethos must encourage self-reliance and responsibility. It is much harder for individual citizens to practice the disciplines of self-restraint and to show resolution in attaining their goals when the ethos around them mocks such efforts. Individual citizens more easily practice personal responsibility when major national and local institutions provide the necessary moral support. On the one hand, a free society recognizes the responsibility of individuals to govern their own lives by the values they choose; on the other hand, government, television, newspapers, universities, the schools, religious institutions, the cinema, popular singers, and neighborhood organizations do not leave the public unaffected by the behaviors they glamorize and the behaviors they mock. Such institutions shape the set of life-stories, symbols, and images that teach a population what sorts of behaviors are expected of them.

For two centuries, the dominant ethos of this nation celebrated self-control, self-mastery, self-determination, and self-reliance. "Confirm thy soul in self-control," a patriotic hymn insisted. For generations, the McGuffey readers taught children the distinctive moral habits expected of American citizens. Older youngsters were taught Emerson's "Self-Reliance" and Thoreau on incorruptible virtue. At the high-tide of the Sunday School Movement, as many as two-thirds of American youngsters were enrolled for "character instruction."[17] That ethos was powerful. It was celebrated in theater, in churches, in schools, and in the early film industry.

For those who were poor under this older ethos, its instruction in character, hard work, duty, and integrity was a lasting boon. To be taught sound habits when one was malleable and open to instruction was of invaluable consequence in later years.

During our lifetime, that ethos has been in significant measure eroded. Self-control and impulse-restraint were debunked as "square." What was once understood as moral law came to be described as "social convention," and defiance of convention was portrayed as cool, brave, and heroic. Impulse-restraint was ridiculed, while impulse-release came to be celebrated. "Self-expression" was portrayed as a higher form of consciousness. Liberation from the "old morality" was presented by some as the highest virtue.

For those of ample means, such cultural rebellion did not always prove to be harmful. To be poor, however, and to accept the incessant barrage of messages exempting the individual from responsibility, from duty, and from self-discipline may profoundly damage one's chances of escaping from poverty. A poverty constituted by moral disorder prejudices the prospects of the individuals affected far more than the disadvantages inherent in the poverty constituted by a low family income alone.

Yet much thinking about poverty for a long time ignored the effects that the recent shift in the national ethos might have upon some of its most vulnerable and needy citizens, especially among the young. Social workers were sometimes taught "not to ask questions about conduct" and to be "nonjudgmental." Government programs offered benefits but insisted upon no accompanying obligations.

Meanwhile, a fever of "liberation" and "impulse-release" has had visible effects upon the behaviors of the impressionable young, not least among the poor.

To imagine that the needs of the poor are material only is to devalue the moral dignity of the poor. Not all who might be eligible for benefits—food stamps, say—take advantage of them; some, perhaps, count the cost in terms of independence lost. One of the moral resources some still call upon is a fierce resistance to dependency. These resources can be undermined by poorly designed efforts to help the poor. The poor themselves are aware of such temptations. According to a *Los Angeles Times* poll in 1985, 64 percent of the poor and 70 percent of poor women say it is "almost always" or "often" true that "poor young women have babies so they can collect welfare" (51 percent of the nonpoor said "seldom" or "almost never"). Welfare "almost always" or "often" encourages husbands to avoid family responsibilities, according to 60 percent of the poor persons polled.[18] By no means all the poor fall victim to such moral hazards. Many accept a hand up, but only long enough to reassert their own independence.

The ethos implicit in government programs ought to encourage, but often does not, those of the dependent who struggle to become self-reliant—an admittedly complex task. For one thing, human personality is marvelously intricate and no two persons are the same. In administering welfare benefits, while encouraging self-reliance, it is particularly difficult to design a suitable transition phase, both for *entry into* a welfare program (under criteria for eligibility) and for *exit from* it back into independence.

Compared with dependency, independence carries costs and hazards. It has its rewards, of course, and most persons (but not all) would prefer to be independent for reasons of personal dignity. The satisfactions that spring from this should not be underestimated. But generations of welfare experience, both in the United States and abroad,[19] have also demonstrated that the availability of public benefits introduces perverse incentives, such as the temptation to forgo independence for security and assured benefits.

Further, poorly designed programs affect not only their recipients but also the morale of the public. Thus, it does not seem fair for one couple to commit itself to hard labor for two incomes at the minimum wage, just enough to disqualify them for various benefits, when they see others work as little as possible in order to secure benefits more generous than their own combined incomes. And even a person on welfare determined to become independent may question whether the take-home pay from working exceeds the loss of a benefit package, particularly its medical coverage.

For many such reasons, the current design of welfare policy often seems to violate the dignity of the poor, because it treats the poor as if they were without responsibility, and therefore as if they were of some lesser moral dignity. Meanwhile, many of our major institutions have contributed to shaping an ethos that, when lived out by the poor, has devastating consequences.

By contrast, a sound ethos would raise hopes for all. As a brave social worker in Newark told Bill Moyers about the need for basic values among the young poor, in a 1985 documentary that attracted much attention, "If you say it in your corner and I say it in my corner, and everybody's saying it, it's going to be like a drumbeat."[20]

All our major national and local institutions have responsibilities to the most vulnerable and needy in our society. Those responsibilities include the shaping of an ethos favorable to those of the poor seeking, often against great odds, to practice the traditional disciplines by which Americans have long bettered their own condition and that of their families. The nobility of those who struggle deserves far more celebration than it receives. Their efforts add to the common good of all, and all are correspondingly in their debt.

The central focus of efforts to reduce poverty should be on families and children. Helping the family is the most sweeping, practical, and profound way of diminishing poverty. Nearly two-thirds of all Americans below the government's poverty line live in families with children under eighteen. Nearly 80 percent live in families.[21] No other institution is so universal and so basic to society. The family is nature's original department of health, education, and human services. When things go well in the family, the whole of society reaps many benefits. When families—in one way or another, for one reason or another—fail to accomplish their basic tasks, it is far harder for other social institutions to accomplish theirs.

A failure to learn the alphabet and the rudiments of reading in the home slows down education in the school; a failure to learn sound habits of nutrition at home lowers the level of public health; a failure to learn habits of self-mastery, work, and citizenship at home leads to habits of nonwork, hustling, or crime. The family is the matrix within which the citizen is well-formed or misshapen. No institution is so important, yet so easily overlooked.

By 1987, emphasis upon the family had become nonpartisan. Both major parties see the need to help and to strengthen the beleaguered family. A group of Democratic officeholders has issued a strong paper: "The Road to Independence: Strengthening America's

Families in Need."[22] Republican emphasis upon family under President Reagan has helped to focus public attention.[23] Both on the left and on the right, writers compete to show concern for family values, income, and welfare.[24] All have learned important lessons from recent history.

In 1962, President John F. Kennedy launched a welfare reform proposal that was to lead eventually to "The War on Poverty." He himself chose to focus on the family in the message he sent to Congress with his reforms:

> . . . our public welfare programs . . . must stress the integrity and preservation of the family unit . . . must contribute to the attack on dependency, juvenile delinquency, family breakdown, illegitimacy, ill health, and disability . . . must reduce the incidence of these problems, prevent their occurrence and recurrence, and strengthen and protect the vulnerable in a highly competitive world.[25]

The president emphasized the family unit in 1962. Yet if one looks at American families twenty-five years later, one will not find that they are more intact or stronger than in 1962, especially among the poor.

On the contrary, the fraction of all families with children that are female-headed has increased from 8 percent in 1962 to 21 percent in 1985. Among poor families with children, the female-headed proportion has risen from 30 percent to 56 percent. The proportion of children born out of wedlock has dramatically increased, from 6 percent to 20 percent. By 1985, female-headed families (3.1 million) and their minor children (6.7 million) had become the single largest block of the population below the government's poverty line, numbering nearly 10 million persons, 30 percent of the total. Along with these are 2.3 million poor husband-wife families with children under eighteen (5.4 million), also nearly 10 million persons.[26]

While its commitment to civil liberties permits wide latitude in matters of personal morality, the nation also promulgates laws that prescribe basic acceptable behaviors regarding the family—and for good reason. Behaviors regarding family life have many practical, public effects. Recent rises in family breakups and out-of-wedlock births have pushed increasing numbers of Americans below the poverty line. Children born out of wedlock face a higher probability of low birthweight and greater health risks than children of married parents. Children in single-parent homes on average perform less well in school and are more likely to drop out from school than children in intact homes. Society bears the costs of such disparities and, in this way, personal decisions end up being concerns of public policy.

Summary

These, then, are the elements of a new consensus. All six of the preceding "starting places" point directly toward the family. Without a growing job market and opportunities for higher wage rates, struggling families find it harder to attain the independence from the state that is their proper station. "Disaggregating the poor" shows that the vast majority of the population below the poverty line lives in families. The successful efforts of the past twenty years have lifted up the older generation of family members, while the new poverty is now more concentrated among younger families. This new poverty seems to include a shift in values affecting the family and to be characterized less by low income alone and more by an increasingly common dependency. Again, the astonishing abandonment of young mothers by males, who beget children without supporting them, has focused national attention upon personal responsibility. With accumulating power, the blurred, sometimes disordered set of expectations for behavior portrayed by our major institutions reaches directly into family homes; one must insist upon personal responsibility and social obligation. Since personal values do not arise in a vacuum, one must attend to the health of the national ethos. (It is not only the physical ether that ought not to be polluted.)

In short, the family is the arena in which the battle to reduce poverty—both in its material and in its moral components—should be most hotly contested.

But now it is time to apply the second of our seven starting points by asking "Who are the poor?" and disaggregating the kinds and types of poverty.

Notes

1. See Charles Murray with Deborah Laren, "According to Age: Longitudinal Profiles of AFDC Recipients and the Poor by Age Group" (Paper presented at the Working Seminar on the Family and American Welfare Policy, Washington, D.C., September 23, 1986, mimeo). This study, commissioned by the Working Seminar, involved a close analysis of the Panel Study of Income Dynamics (PSID) at the University of Michigan. Murray reports as follows:

> The PSID reveals with striking clarity that the requirements for getting out of poverty in this country are so minimal that it takes a mutually reinforcing cluster of behaviors to remain in poverty, even if you are black and even if you are female. If you follow a set of modest requirements, you are almost surely going to avoid poverty.

These requirements for a male, black or white, are to go to a free public school and complete high school. Get into the labor market and get a job, any job, and stick with the labor market. Do so, and the odds that you will be poor are small. If you are poor, the odds that you will not only get out of poverty but get comfortably out of poverty are very large. Consider: Of all men ages 20-64 with just a high school education, only six-tenths of one percent were in poverty in 1970. Even for blacks, only 4.7 percent of male heads of household with just a high school education were even in near-poverty by 1980. Among adult males with just a high school education of all races, 91 percent had family incomes greater than twice the poverty level. Among adult black males, 86 percent had family incomes greater than twice the poverty level . . . .

For women, the aggregate odds are not so different. Again using adult women with just a high school education as the benchmark, only 2 percent of all of them were in poverty as of 1970. For black women, the figure was much higher: 8.5 percent. But it is higher primarily by comparison. How many people, asked to estimate the economic status of black women with just a high school education, would have had the temerity to assert that more than 90 percent are above the poverty line?

2. Alice M. Rivlin, ed., *Economic Choices 1984* (Washington, D.C.: Brookings Institution, 1984), p. 2.

3. According to census figures, only 59.7 percent of U.S. homes had their own indoor flush toilets in 1940; by 1980, only 2.7 percent lacked complete indoor plumbing. U.S. Department of Commerce, Bureau of the Census, *Sixteenth Census of the United States, 1940: Housing,* vol. 2, table 7A; *idem,* Current Housing Reports, H-150-80, *Annual Housing Survey: 1980,* part E: Urban and Rural Housing Characteristics (Washington, D.C.: U.S. Government Printing Office, 1983), table A-1.

4. U.S. National Center for Health Statistics, *Vital Statistics of the United States* (annual).

5. Public Health Service, Indian Health Service, *Chart Series Book, April 1986,* p. 22.

6. Mary Jo Bane, "Testimony before the House Select Committee on Hunger," August 5, 1986.

7. U.S. Department of Commerce, Bureau of the Census, Current Population Reports, Series P-60, Number 154, *Money Income and Poverty Status of Families and Persons in the United States: 1985 (Advance Data from the March 1986 Current Population Survey)* (Washington, D.C.: U.S. Government Printing Office, 1986), table 16.

8. U.S. Department of Commerce, Bureau of the Census, Technical Paper 56, *Estimates of Poverty Including the Value of Noncash Benefits: 1985* (Washington, D.C.: U.S. Government Printing Office, 1986), table A; and U.S., Social Security Administration, *Annual Statistical Supplement to the Social Security*

Bulletin (Washington, D.C.: U.S. Government Printing Office, 1986).

9. *Estimates of Poverty Including Noncash Benefits 1985*, table 4. In the Census Bureau methodology, the value assigned to Medicare and Medicaid benefits is *not* their cost to the government—which would be unfair to persons with high medical costs—but rather the value to the individual of an equivalent private insurance policy. For the methodology by which medical and other noncash benefits are valued, see the Introduction to *Estimates of Poverty Including Noncash Benefits 1985*.

10. Calculated from *Money Income and Poverty Status 1985*, table 21.

11. Counting both means-tested and non-means-tested aid, the noncash benefit total (in 1985 dollars) was $6.4 billion in 1965; $127 billion in 1985. U.S. Department of Commerce, Bureau of the Census, Technical Paper 57, *Estimates of Poverty Including the Value of Noncash Benefits: 1979 to 1982*, table A; and *Estimates of Poverty Including Noncash Benefits 1985*, table A.

12. *Money Income and Poverty Status 1985*, table 16; and *Estimates of Poverty Including Noncash Benefits 1985*, table 1.

13. *Money Income and Poverty Status 1985*, table 18.

14. Daniel Patrick Moynihan, "Welfare Reform's 1971–72 Defeat: A Historic Loss," *Journal of the Institute for Socioeconomic Studies*, vol. 6 (Spring 1981), p. 8. See also Karl Zinsmeister, "The Poverty Problem of the Eighties," *Public Opinion*, June/July 1985.

15. U.S. National Center for Health Statistics, *Vital Statistics of the United States* (annual). In AFDC families, for instance, 46 percent of children under 18 were born to unmarried mothers. U.S. Department of Health and Human Services, Family Support Administration, Office of Family Assistance, *Recipient Characteristics and Financial Circumstances of AFDC Recipients*, 1983 (mimeo), p. 2; also, table 15.

16. For a detailed discussion of these mutual obligations, see Lawrence Mead, *Beyond Entitlement: The Social Obligations of Citizenship* (New York: Free Press, 1986), chapter 2; and Mead, "The Work Problem in Welfare" (Paper presented at the Working Seminar on the Family and American Welfare Policy, Washington, D.C., October 11, 1986, mimeo).

17. See James Q. Wilson, "The Rediscovery of Character," *The Public Interest*, vol. 81 (Fall 1985): "In this country as well as in England, a variety of enterprises—Sunday schools, public schools, temperance movements, religious revivals, YMCAs, the Children's Aid Society—were launched in the first half of the twentieth century that had in common the goal of instilling a 'self-activating, self-regulating, all-purpose inner control.' . . . We lack any reliable measure of the effects of these efforts, save one—the extraordinary reduction in the per capita consumption of alcoholic beverages that occurred between 1830 (when the temperance efforts began in earnest) and 1850 and that persisted (despite an upturn during and just after the Civil War) for the rest of the century . . . . Some great benefits have flowed from . . . [the change from self-control to self-expression] but the costs are just as real, at least for those young persons who have not already acquired a decent degree of self-restraint and other-regardingness" (p. 13).

18. I. A. Lewis and William Schneider, "Hard Times: The Public on Poverty," *Public Opinion*, June/July 1985, table 1.

19. See Leslie Lenkowsky, *Politics, Economics, and Welfare Reform: The Failure of the Negative Income Tax in Britain and the United States* (Lanham, Maryland: AEI/University Press of America, 1986): "The way recipients (or potential recipients) have responded to particular programs has often been more significant than what the program is actually designed to achieve. In the past, people have been thought to move from county to county, to quit their jobs, and to abandon their families in order to obtain higher benefits. In the Irish case, the availability of pensions even caused a portion of the population to 'become' older" (p. 35). For another view, see Michael B. Katz, *In the Shadow of the Poor House: A Social History of Welfare in America* (New York: Basic Books, 1986).

20. Carolyn Wallace, quoted on "The Vanishing Family—Crisis in Black America," CBS Television, reported by Bill Moyers, January 25, 1986.

21. *Money Income and Poverty Status 1985*, table 16; *Estimates of Poverty Including Noncash Benefits 1985*, table 2.

22. The Social Policy Task Force, *The Road to Independence: Strengthening America's Families in Need* (Washington, D.C.: National Legislative Educational Foundation, 1986): "A primary goal of social policy must be to enable government to assist families and children—and especially poor families and children—in ways that help to strengthen these families. Any policy should have at its core the achievement of family self-sufficiency, the promotion and the health and well-being of children, and the elimination of barriers that keep people from reaching their potential" (p. 8).

23. See, for example, the report of the Domestic Policy Council's Working Group on the Family, Gary Bauer, chairman, "The Family: Preserving America's Future" (mimeo). "Family" was the first of the five points Ronald Reagan stressed in his 1980 presidential campaign: "Family, work, neighborhood, peace, and freedom."

24. See, *inter alia*, Jack A. Meyer, ed., *Ladders Out of Poverty: A Report of the Project on the Welfare of Families*, Bruce Babbitt and Arthur Flemming, co-chairs (Washington, D.C.: American Horizons, 1986); American Public Welfare Association and the National Council of State Human Service Administrators, *One Child in Four* (1986); National Governors' Association, Welfare Prevention Task Force Report, (forthcoming); Irwin Garfinckel and Susan McLanahan, *Single Mothers and Their Children: A New American Dilemma* (Washington, D.C.: Urban Institute, 1986); and New York State Task Force on Poverty and Welfare, "A New Social Contract: Rethinking the Nature and Purpose of Public Assistance," submitted to Gov. Mario M. Cuomo, December 1986.

25. John F. Kennedy, "Special Message to the Congress on Public Welfare Programs," *Public Papers of the Presidents of the United States* (Washington, D.C.: Office of the *Federal Register*, National Archives and Record Service, 1953–), pp. 102–103.

26. U.S. Department of Commerce, Bureau of the Census, *U.S. Census of Population*, 1960, vol. 1; idem, Current Population Reports, Series P-20, no.

411, *Household and Family Characteristics: March 1985,* table F; idem, *Characteristics of the Population Below the Poverty Level: 1984,* table 4; U.S. National Center for Health Statistics, *Vital Statistics of the United States* (annual); *Estimates of Poverty Including Noncash Benefits 1985,* table 2.

PART TWO

Who Are the Poor? Who Are the Dependent?

The imposition of an obligation actually shows respect for the recipient, it enhances the dignity of such persons. By holding up a common standard of behavior to all able-bodied citizens we evidence our confidence that those who may now need our assistance are capable of becoming self-reliant. This avoids the situation in which "we," who are capable of responsible conduct and of generosity, deign to provide for "them" who, by virtue of their dependency are rendered objects of our concern, but are not treated as responsible moral agents.

GLENN C. LOURY

2

Disaggregating the Poor

Beyond Conventional Categories

From the outset, the Working Seminar set out to review the literature on poverty and to reexamine the conventional ways of understanding it. Every road kept leading us back to the stubborn fact of dependency, constituted in part by behavioral components, and to the central role of family life.

In one sense, this line of reflection showed that the magnitude of worst-case poverty is smaller than we are often led to think, because the most damaging forms of dependency affect only a portion (although a significant and growing portion) of the poor. In another sense, that problem is so severe, complex, and deep that overcoming it will not be easy or quick. There is no silver bullet. There is no one simple thing to do. Immense patience and perseverance will be necessary, and the maturity of the nation itself will be tested.

It is often said, for example, that children now constitute almost 40 percent of the poor, and they do. But this way of stating the problem overlooks the fact that a solid majority (57 percent) of children in households below the official poverty line are living with only one parent and that a very high fraction have been born out of wedlock. Their future prospects are affected not solely by living in a family of low income, but by living in a family circumstance empirically associated with unusual social, medical, and moral hazards. Finding ways to come to the aid of such threatened youngsters will not be easy, but to do so is a challenge the nation must meet.

Similarly, the nation's most vivid images of poverty are offered on television and in color photographs in the news magazines. These are usually images of blacks or Hispanics on the mean streets of densely poor urban ghettos. Only a small fraction of all blacks and Hispanics are both poor and concentrated in those census tracts in the nation's 100 largest central cities in which at least 20 percent of the inhabitants are below the government's poverty line. But the dependency of the 5 million or so who are in that situation is of a depth not exhausted by the catch-all phrase "below the official poverty line."[1]

In order to grasp this point firmly, however, it is highly useful to begin with the more or less conventional official description of poverty and to subject it to a more penetrating analysis. Behind its bland descriptions lie sometimes shocking realities.

It is well known that the official poverty measure, in use since 1964, is limited in what it can tell us.[2] It is based upon estimates of current annual income, which are far less revealing than the more detailed measures of actual expenditures that are also available.[3] It counts only *cash* income, ignoring the large panoply of noncash benefits that government has made available, as well as the at times substantial personal assets that individuals with low cash incomes may have.[4] It counts only *pretax* income, thus disguising year-to-year differences that arise from changes in tax policy (this will become especially important as the 1986 tax law takes effect). It especially disguises the effect of increasingly high payroll taxes for social security.[5] It takes no account of the underreporting of income. It takes no account of wide disparities of living costs within this continental-sized nation, as between regions and between urban and rural ways of life. It is, further, routinely adjusted by methods that remain an issue of serious technical dispute. Above all, the official poverty line can reveal nothing at all about the behavioral dimensions of dependency.

Nonetheless, since the convention of using the official poverty line is well entrenched and has some value in tracking trends over time, we open our discussion in the conventional way, but only in order to go beyond it speedily. Although we will keep referring to the official poverty line throughout part two, our true focus is on behavioral dependency.

Thus, table 2–1 displays the two most telling Census Bureau measures, one for cash income only and the other including the "market value" of noncash benefits such as food stamps. Although the second measure is also vulnerable to specific criticisms, the difference between the two offers dramatic evidence that noncash benefits have considerable effect. "Market-valued" noncash benefits reduce the official count of persons in poverty from about 33 to 22 million; the number of poor families from just over 7 million to just under 5 million; and the number of the elderly poor from 3.5 to 0.9 million.

The figures in table 2–1 also show that, under both measures, about four-fifths of the poverty population lives in families; that, depending on the measure, about half of these families are headed by a single parent; and that about two-fifths of the official poverty population are children under eighteen.

TABLE 2–1

POPULATION BELOW THE U.S. POVERTY LINE, 1985

	Cash Income Only		After Noncash Benefits[a]	
	Number (millions)	Percent of poor	Number (millions)	Percent of poor
Individuals				
Total	33.1	100	21.9	100
In families	25.7	78	17.1	78
In families with children under 18	20.3	62	13.7	63
Unrelated individuals	6.7	20	4.3	20
Over 64	3.5	10	0.9	4
Under 18	13.0	39	8.8	40
Families				
Total	7.2	100	4.7	100
Married couple	3.4	47	2.4	51
Single-headed	3.8	53	2.3	49

a. At "market value," excluding institutional expenditures.

SOURCE: U.S. Bureau of the Census, *Money Income and Poverty Status of Families and Persons in the U.S., 1985*; and *Estimates of Poverty Including the Value of Noncash Benefits: 1985*.

We begin with a brief comparison of the poor with the nonpoor. Then we turn to the elderly, for whose care there is already an express national policy: their poverty, in the view of the public, should be reduced as close to zero as is humanly possible. Their dependency, on account of age, is thought to be wholly legitimate, and all of them ought to be able to live out the remainder of their lives in decent circumstances.

Next we turn to the 6.7 million or 4.3 million (whichever the measure) "unrelated individuals" whose cash or noncash benefits still leave them below the poverty line. Within this group, we focus next on young black males ages sixteen to twenty-four. Many among them are doing well, but a significant proportion are not.

Since the most visible of these young black males live in poverty areas in central cities, they further draw our attention to the recently named "underclass," whose special problems of behavioral dependency lie at the heart of the nation's current concern.

Having considered the smaller subgroups among the conventionally defined poor, we turn next to the families of the poor. We begin with husband-wife families among the poor, whose chances both of exiting from poverty and of weathering it with more abundant resources are high. Since 7.1 million of the nation's 13 million children below the poverty line live in single-parent households, however, the weight of our study lies with them.[6]

Finally, we turn to aspects of the condition of the poor that frequently fail to be brought into discussion, but whose cumulative effect on the daily lives of the dependent poor, in particular, is oftentimes crushing: such factors include geographical concentration, inadequate and abused housing, low participation in the labor force, low rates of full-time employment, and acute violations of the rights of the poor to integrity of life, limb, and property through daily vulnerability to criminal assault.

The human condition of the dependent poor sometimes lies hidden behind the veil of conventional statistical surveys. We try to penetrate that veil.

Focusing on the Dependent

Who Are the Nonpoor? It is a little surprising that statistical surveys reveal so many differences between the poor and the nonpoor. The natural instinct of Americans is to treat everyone alike. Indeed, many of the poor of yesterday are today among the nonpoor; and some of the nonpoor today may through some happenstance become poor tomorrow. As Greg Duncan and others have shown, there is great churning in the American social system.[7] On the one hand, individuals through their own choices profoundly affect their own life chances; on the other hand, events beyond their control may suddenly alter their condition. Persistent success is by no means guaranteed for anyone. Nonetheless, in certain respects, significant differences between the poor and the nonpoor appear in statistical snapshots of both.

On the one side, for example, the median age of the nonpoor, thirty-three, is considerably higher than that of the poor, twenty-three.[8] This is not surprising, since most persons have lower incomes at a younger age, higher when older, and add children to their families while they are still young—but it is, just the same, a significant difference. On the other side, and contrary to myth, the average number of children in poor families, 2.2, is not greatly higher than in nonpoor families, 1.8—although even this difference means that the former are growing in number, the latter just about standing still.[9]

Telling differences appear in home ownership, education, and marital status. A surprising 41 percent of the poor own their own homes, compared with 74 percent of the nonpoor.[10] Some 45 percent of poor adults have completed high school, whereas 66 percent of the nonpoor have.[11] About one-third of the nonpoor have completed college, while the relatively fewer college graduates who are counted as poor include in their number graduate students and early retirees.[12] Only 38 percent of poor adults are married, compared with 66 percent of the nonpoor.[13] As we shall see in more detail later, the labor force participation rate of the able poor is far lower than that of the nonpoor, and so is their rate of full-time, year-round employment.[14]

Just over 19 million of the nonpoor lived in female-headed families in 1983.[15] But female-headed families (totaling 11.6 million persons) account for nearly half of all poor families. Being born out of wedlock also raises one's chances of being poor. Among the 7.0 million children on AFDC in 1983 (the most recent reporting year), 3.1 million (46 percent) had parents who were not joined in wedlock.[16]

All these factors—age, home ownership, education, marital status, and full-time, year-round employment—differentiate the poor from the nonpoor. To complete high school, to work consistently full time year round (even at a minimum-wage job), and to be and to stay married are characteristics statistically correlated with avoiding poverty.[17] These are demanding, although not superhuman, tasks. To neglect them—to drop out of school, to work irregularly, to remain unmarried, and to have children out of wedlock—is to raise one's chances (and one's children's chances) of living in poverty.

We need now to consider the involuntary dependency of some of the elderly poor, which is quite different in kind from behavioral dependency.

The Elderly. Twenty years ago, the most touching symbol of poverty was the elderly man or woman, typically shown outside a rural shack. In 1966 the elderly constituted 18 percent of the poverty population; and 29 percent of those sixty-five and over were poor. Thanks to systematic raises in social security payments and the institution of payments through the Supplemental Security Income (SSI) program, and thanks also to higher enrollments in private pension funds, the elderly today are in a significantly better cash position. By 1985 the elderly constituted 10 percent of the poverty population, and the poverty rate for the elderly (13 percent) was *below* the national poverty rate. When noncash benefits to the elderly—food stamps, housing assistance, and above all the insurance value of Medicare—are counted at "market value," the poverty rate of the elderly falls to about 3 percent (see table 2–1), although some qualifications are needed.[18] But even this does not tell the whole story.

For many reasons, including scientific advances, the elderly are now enjoying unprecedented longevity. Because of Medicare, most of the elderly poor have access to standards of medical care never before available. Accordingly, the number of persons over sixty-five has grown dramatically since 1960 (from about 17 million to about 29 million in 1985). Meanwhile, their political clout has grown as their proportion of the population grew from 9 percent in 1960 to 12 percent in 1985.[19]

Furthermore, the official poverty figures understate the advances of the elderly because they measure only annual cash income, whereas older persons can also draw on accumulated assets. About 75 percent of the elderly own their own homes, nearly all of these paid for, and the rapid appreciation of real estate during the past decades has generally outstripped inflation. Even among the elderly *poor*, a quarter have net home equity of $50,000 or more.[20]

These achievements, however, mask other problems. The great gains in longevity, particularly for women, have as a not-so-hidden cost the increased need for nursing homes and other forms of long-term care, when the "elderly-elderly" (as the increasing numbers of those over seventy-five have come to be called) become less able to care for themselves. These forms of care are increasingly expensive. Turning to them typically means being uprooted from family, friends, and familiar surroundings. In fact, nearly 60 percent of the elderly poor (1.9 million) lived alone in 1984.[21]

Both because elderly women are poorer than elderly men and because women (whether widowed or divorced) on average live longer than men, among the poor past their sixty-fifth birthday an astonishing 71 percent are women. (Among the elderly who are *not* poor, there are also more women than men, but by a far smaller margin.) Similarly, among the 1.9 million elderly poor living alone, only 300,000 are males.[22] Because of the way social security was originally designed and because many older women were not employed for pay in the proportions younger women now are (and so did not build up social security credits), many elderly women receive lower benefits than elderly men. Among black women over sixty-five and living alone, the 1985 poverty rate was 55 percent.[23] Social security was not designed as a poverty program; however, a federal program of income supplements for the elderly poor (SSI) has been added to it for this purpose.[24] Thus, the nation has in place programs capable, in principle, of reducing poverty among the elderly to zero. Since some of the elderly may be isolated and overlooked, to make sure that all who need assistance receive it remains to be accomplished.

In sum, most of the elderly support themselves out of their accumulated social security benefits, pensions, and assets. Many are also supported by their families, religious institutions, or other private sources. Those who lack such supports are dependent almost solely upon government programs. Because of the advanced age of the elderly, in keeping with immemorial ethical values, the public has expressly willed that all be so entitled. Their dependency is of a special kind.

Unrelated Individuals. In 1985, by the larger of the two official measures displayed in table 2–1, only 6.7 million of the poor were adult "unrelated individuals." Four million of these lived alone.[25]

Between 1970 and 1985, as marriages were delayed or never formed, and as male-female differences in longevity increased, the number of unrelated individuals soared. While the poverty rate of singles fell, it remains very high, 22 percent.[26]

In the eighteen to twenty-four age bracket, the poverty rate for singles is conspicuously high, just above 32 percent (compared with 14 percent for those ages twenty-five to forty-four).[27] Although their aggregate numbers are not large, poverty for singles ages sixteen to thirty-four, especially in urban settings, is associated with unusually high unemployment. In central cities such as those of New York and Chicago, young singles have become since 1980 the fastest growing segment in the welfare population.[28] In urban settings, behavioral problems such as lack of guidance, noncompletion of high school, nonwork, "hustling," drug abuse, and criminal activity especially afflict the young. But sudden unemployment has also left some older singles in poverty.[29]

For able-bodied unrelated individuals of working age, a full-time job at the minimum wage is sufficient to lift income well above the poverty line of approximately $5,500. This visible solution is, perhaps, why public policy analysts have paid relatively little attention to poor singles. Those among them who are elderly and those who are disabled are commonly covered under special programs. But those between eighteen and thirty-four, who in the past would have been gaining work experience, developing sound habits, and starting families of their own, invite especially vigorous attention.

The Young Black Male. One of the groups with greatest risk of poverty is young black males ages sixteen to twenty-four. There is much concern for children, but this age group, especially the young males—so full of energy and possibility, yet often unsettled—was for a long time overlooked. Until recently, researchers had to look far and wide to find materials on them. Even for census takers, young black males are one of the hardest populations to locate with certainty. Their places of residence may shift back and forth between the dwellings of their parents (or parent), their relatives, and their friends. By the best estimate of the Census Bureau, the total population of black males ages sixteen to twenty-four for 1985 came to 2.5 million.[30]

Here again, we would like to stress the positive. Piecing together a composite for the year 1985, we find that of the 2.5 million black males ages sixteen to twenty-four, some 647,000 (26 percent) were in high school, 351,000 (14 percent) were in college, and 163,000 (7 percent) were in the armed forces.[31] Just over 1 million (40 percent) were employed, and 417,000 (17 percent) were unemployed. On the negative side, 113,000 (5 percent) were in prison or jail.[32] (Numbers do not correspond with totals because of overlaps; for example, among those employed and in college.)

A figure often cited in the media, "the black teen-age unemployment rate" (recently about 35 percent), should be treated with caution, because most teen-agers are still in high school and seeking part-time work, looking for a first job, and the like. The actual number of unemployed black teen-agers (ages sixteen to nineteen) was lower than most people imagine—about 290,000 at the end of 1986, counting both males and females.[33] Nonetheless, the labor force participation rate of all black males ages sixteen to twenty-four has dropped from its level of twenty-five years ago, and only 44 percent of young black males are now employed, compared with 59 percent in 1962 (see table 2–2).[34] Changes in patterns for educational enrollment cannot account for this decline.

TABLE 2–2

BLACK YOUTH EMPLOYMENT, 1970 AND 1985

	Percent Employed	
	1970	1985
Black males		
Ages 18 and 19	51	36
Ages 20 to 24	77	60

SOURCE: Richard B. Freeman, "Cutting Black Youth Unemployment," *New York Times*, July 20, 1986.

The marriage rates of young black males are at historically low levels: 93 percent of them are "never married," compared with 83 percent for white youths of the same age. In 1960 the numbers of married youths of both races were significantly higher, and there was little difference between the races: 74 percent of young white males and 76 percent of young nonwhite males were "never married."[35]

In 1985, Richard B. Freeman and Harry J. Holzer edited an important book reporting on a major survey of this vulnerable and important population, *The Black Youth Unemployment Crisis*.[36] Freeman summarizes his concern:

> Lacking skills and facing a desperate shortage of jobs with career prospects, many young black men consider street life an attractive and rational alternative to the normal working world. Many have serious drug and drinking problems, and are deeply involved in crime—in 1980, according to Census Bureau figures, more than 4 percent of black men aged 20 to 29 were in jail. Many more simply waste their youth hanging around street corners.[37]

Nearly one-half of sixteen-to-twenty-four-year-old black men had no work experience at all in 1984.[38] The startling decline in their condition between 1970 and 1985 is represented in table 2–2. Freeman and his associates, analyzing extensive surveys and interviews conducted in inner-city poverty areas in Boston, Philadelphia, and Chicago, find "no single cause" of this decline in employment. "Rather," he writes, "joblessness among young black men is part-and-parcel of other social pathologies that go beyond the labor market, including youth crime, and drug and alcohol abuse, residual employer discrimination and performance on the job, particularly absenteeism."[39]

These youths do not appear to be unwilling to work. Asked to pick from a list of hourly wages at which they would find work "acceptable," the inner-city black youngsters, on average, chose an hourly wage level ($4.47) twelve cents lower than that chosen by average unemployed white youths, but well above the minimum wage ($3.35). They were

> generally unwilling to take worse or lower-paying jobs despite higher unemployment . . . . Black youths were half as likely to find work in a two-week period than were white youths. When out of work, moreover, the typical inner-city black youth was more likely to spend his time hanging out or watching TV than engaging in activities likely to enhance job prospects.[40]

Indeed, the average black youngster, out of school and unemployed, spent only 9 percent of his time on anything that researchers judged could plausibly be described as socially useful or self-improving.[41]

Some 32 percent of youths surveyed thought they could earn more from criminal "street" activity than from legitimate work. Twenty-one percent admitted to drug use beyond marijuana. These same youths had "markedly lower" chances of being in school or holding a job.[42]

The researchers also found that "youth joblessness is connected to the family's welfare status." Here is Freeman's summary:

> Black youths from welfare homes with the same family income and otherwise comparable to youths from non-welfare homes had a much worse experience in the job market. Youths living in public housing projects also did less well than youths living in private housing. Thus, the unemployment rate among 19- to 24-year-olds who received no public assistance and who did not live in public housing was 28 percent in 1979. Among those from families on welfare, the unemployment rate rose to 43.8 percent. And among those whose families collected welfare and lived in public housing, the unemployment rate soared to 52 percent.[43]

Current welfare programs appear to do little to correct these problems. To do so, they would have to go beyond financial assistance to questions of ethos and morale.

Many of the most violence-prone of these youngsters, Freeman notes, have already dropped out or been expelled from school. For them, the "noisy, chaotic and crime-ridden environment of public housing projects" become magnets. This "is not, to say the least, an atmosphere in which middle class [and working class] values about work can take hold."[44]

Against such odds, however, other black youths were patiently building the habits and skills necessary to escape from poverty. Freeman sketches their profile in broad outline. For one thing, they went to church far more often. Of those who did not go to church, 24 percent admitted committing an illegal act during the past twelve months, 46 percent used drugs, and only 45 percent were in school. Among those who attended church once a week or more, the profile was significantly more hopeful: an illegal act, 12 percent; drug use, 21 percent; and in school, 71 percent.[45]

Furthermore, youths from families in which other persons worked also tended to do better in the job market. The reasons may be because they have access to better family information and family "connections" in finding jobs, and may enjoy "a stronger work ethic instilled by the family experience."[46]

Moreover, surprisingly, 71 percent of the youths neither in school nor employed said they could obtain a minimum-wage job very or somewhat easily. "The problem," Freeman writes, "is not one of creating jobs, but of creating jobs that offer career opportunities that dominate alternative opportunities, such as crime."[47] Freeman clearly means *real* jobs, not make-work; as always he speaks in the context of "a stronger work ethic."

In Chicago, at the borderline between black and white neighborhoods, "the white youths got the jobs," suggesting that "race, education and cultural factors," not location, are what count. The importance of location was further diminished by the finding that "black youths living in Chicago close to factories and jobs had only marginally better employment experience than those living far away from jobs."[48]

Freeman and his associates put significant weight on the need for the whole range of public and private social responses to this many-faceted disorder. These would include responses from schools, churches, employers, and community organizations, as well as from the welfare and criminal justice system.

The period from 1965 on was certainly more favorable to black advancement than any preceding period. In general, most blacks, including young black males, did improve their condition: in education, income, opportunity, and social mobility. But among the 2.5 million single black males ages sixteen to twenty-four, a significant fraction suffers from dependencies from which their brothers have freed themselves. These dependencies seem more deeply rooted and fundamental than before. An increasing proportion, born out of wedlock, have lacked a father's guidance, discipline, and counsel. Some have prematurely become fathers themselves, before having the moral and financial resources to meet responsibilities for which they may have had no intimate model.

The Urban Underclass. The most vivid form of poverty in the United States is geographically concentrated within the nation's largest cities. Increasingly, economic growth and antidiscrimination efforts have enabled many upwardly mobile families and individuals to leave such areas. Many of those left behind are, in the words of William Julius Wilson, "persons who lack training and skills and either experience long-term unemployment or have dropped out of the labor force altogether; who are long-term public assistance recipients; and who are engaged in street criminal activity and other forms of aberrant behavior."[49] This concentrated population is increasingly black and

Hispanic. Using recently released figures from the 1980 census, Richard Nathan and John Lago have calculated that in the nation's 100 largest cities there were 4.1 million poor blacks and Hispanics concentrated in census tracts in which 20 percent or more of the population was in poverty.[50] Troublingly, Nathan and Lago found that the minority poverty population in the nation's largest cities increased substantially over the 1970s and became more concentrated in poverty tracts.[51]

Since this concentrated urban population seems unusually resistant to economic growth, and since it runs against the grain of a traditional American sense of opportunity, upward mobility, and classlessness, both popular writers and social scientists have felt driven to describe it in the new and deliberately shocking term "underclass."[52] The conditions that characterize this class, Nathan writes, are "economic, behavioral and geographically focused."[53] These conditions include attitudinal factors such as a sense of alienation from society's norms and values, sometimes aggressive and exploitative behaviors toward others, and sometimes what Thomas Pettigrew calls a "learned helplessness."[54] Its problems extend far beyond economic factors. Thus, among most writers, there is consensus that participation in the values, norms, behaviors, and activities necessary for economic success offers the only real solution to dependency.

Among the highlights of the 1980 Census Bureau data, the following stand out. In 1980, the nation's 100 largest cities contained 8.1 million persons classified as poor, some 17 percent of their population; 3.7 million were black; 3.4 million were white; persons of other races made up the remaining million. About a third of these poor were dispersed throughout their cities, but about two-thirds were concentrated in census tracts where at least 20 percent of the population was below the poverty line. This concentration was twice as great for blacks: 83 percent of poor blacks lived in poverty tracts, compared with 41 percent of poor whites.[55]

Several characteristics of the concentrated poor stand out. The proportion of female-headed households is stunningly high: 74 percent for blacks, 55 percent for Hispanics, 49 percent for whites. In urban poverty areas, poverty is overwhelmingly related to marital status.[56]

Work records also stand out. The unemployment rate for poor persons in high-poverty tracts is more than three times as high as for all income groups citywide: 24.8 percent versus 7.4 percent. The unemployment rate for poor blacks is especially high: 30.3 percent, compared with 17.5 percent for poor whites. Most of those who do work work only part time or during part of the year.[57]

These figures prompt the observation that in poverty areas in the nation's 100 largest cities, two pillars of the traditional ethic appear to have broken down: the husband-wife family and regular, full-time work. But even this is only part of the story. Significant numbers among the underclass are hardly prepared to work, having but poor mastery of the relevant skills, habits, and attitudes.

Although the population of urban poverty areas represents only a fraction of all the poor, it is situated near the major centers of communication and is by far the most visible. No doubt its high visibility colors the way the nation thinks about poverty. Its condition, therefore, has weakened the early confidence of the 1960s that economic growth and equal opportunity would alone suffice to eliminate poverty. More to the point, its current condition has weakened the earlier consensus that assistance to the poor should be value free, since attitudes, habits, and behaviors seem to be constituent factors in the current condition of the underclass. As Glenn Loury writes:

> For a significant proportion of recipients, their dependency is not a short-term circumstance engendered by fortuitous events beyond their control, but rather is a long-term condition arising from behaviors for which they might appropriately be held accountable.[58]

How to help needy and vulnerable persons to become accountable, through participating in the common work of the community, is the present challenge in the nation's new effort to diminish poverty.

Notes

1. Richard P. Nathan, "The Underclass: Will It Always Be with Us?" (Paper presented at the New School for Social Research, November 14, 1986), p. 6, mimeo, p. 2.

2. See Leslie Lenkowsky, "The Concept of Poverty" (Paper presented at the American Enterprise Institute's Public Policy Week, December 1985), mimeo:

> Now and in the past, poverty has been thought of as a matter of insufficient resources, measured in terms of a "poverty-line." Those who lacked the requisite amount were deemed poor and worthy objects of public concern . . . . As a statistical construct for identifying the number of people with low incomes, this conception may still be helpful. But as a way of describing what is most important about the poor, it obscures at least as much as it reveals (p. 2).

See also John Weicher, "Mismeasuring Poverty and Progress" (Paper presented at the American Enterprise Institute's Public Policy Week, Washington, D.C., December 1985), mimeo, revised April 15, 1986; and U.S. House of

Representatives, Committee on Postal Service and Civil Service, Subcommittee on Census and Population, *Summary of Remarks*, August 6 and September 30, 1986.

3. See Nicholas Eberstadt, "Economic and Material Poverty in Modern America" (Paper presented at the Working Seminar on the Family and American Welfare Policy, Washington, D.C., November 9, 1986), pp. 38–39, mimeo.

4. The federal government disbursed $56 billion in means-tested, noncash benefits to the poor in 1985. See the discussion in part one, chapter 1, of this volume. For general discussions of noncash benefits, as well as technical discussions of issues relating to their valuation, see U.S. Department of Commerce, Bureau of the Census, Introductions to Technical Papers 50 through 56, 1982 through 1986.

5. See Eugene Steuerle, "The Tax Treatment of Households of Different Size," in Rudolph G. Penner, ed., *Taxing the Family* (Washington, D.C.: American Enterprise Institute, 1983); and Eugene Steuerle and Paul Wilson, "The Taxation of Poor and Lower Income Workers," in Jack A. Meyer, ed., *Ladders Out of Poverty: A Report of the Project on the Welfare of Families,* Bruce Babbitt and Arthur Flemming, co-chairs (Washington, D.C.: American Horizons, 1986), p. 33:

> Low-income workers often receive little or nothing from transfer and welfare programs, and they usually fail to qualify for any favored tax category; by contrast, the non-working elderly, those who can defer income recognition, or those with general nontaxable fringe benefits are more favorably treated with regard to tax preferences. When the implicit tax rates from the phasing out of welfare and other transfer programs are combined with the implicit and explicit tax rates in the direct tax programs, these low-wage workers often face higher marginal tax rates than most other groups in society.

See also our discussion in part two, chapter 3, of this volume, under the heading "The husband-wife family" and accompanying notes 9 and 10.

6. U.S. Department of Commerce, Bureau of the Census, Technical Paper 56, *Estimates of Poverty Including the Value of Noncash Benefits: 1985* (Washington, D.C.: U.S. Government Printing Office, 1986), table 2.

7. See Greg J. Duncan et al., *Years of Poverty, Years of Plenty* (Ann Arbor, Mich.: Institute for Social Research, 1984). Charles Murray has shown that the income churning, while substantial, is not as arbitrary as it may seem. It is closely related to the changing educational and work experiences of persons as they age. He illustrates this point with his own personal economic history: he went from the bottom income quintile while a graduate student to the top quintile just seven years later when he began working. This fairly predictable and unexceptional pattern—and its reverse later in life—look like turmoil when viewed statistically. Charles Murray with Deborah Laren, "According to Age: Longitudinal Profiles of AFDC Recipients and the Poor by Age Group" (Paper presented at the Working Seminar on the Family and American Welfare Policy, Washington, D.C., September 23, 1986), p. 2, mimeo.

8. Calculated from *Characteristics of the Population below the Poverty Level: 1984* (Washington, D.C.: U.S. Government Printing Office, 1986), table 28.

9. Calculated from U.S. Department of Commerce, Bureau of the Census, *Current Population Reports*, P-60, No. 154, *Money Income and Poverty Status of Families and Persons in the United States: 1985 (Advance Data from the March 1986 Current Population Survey)* (Washington, D.C.: U.S. Government Printing Office, 1986), table 19.

10. Calculated from *Characteristics of the Population below the Poverty Level: 1983*, table 23.

11. Calculated from *Characteristics of the Population below the Poverty Level: 1984*, table 9.

12. Ibid.

13. Calculated from *Characteristics of the Population below the Poverty Level: 1983*, table 21.

14. In 1984, 71 percent of nonpoor persons age fifteen and older worked, compared with 41 percent of poor adults. (Another 6 percent said they wanted to work but were unable to find employment at any time during the year.) Forty-three percent of the nonpoor were employed full time, year round, versus 9 percent of the poor. The disparity in work patterns between the poor and the nonpoor exists even if one excludes the elderly, disabled, and other population groups who have trouble working. See *Characteristics of the Population below the Poverty Level: 1984*, table 10.

15. The poverty rate for female-headed families is 34 percent. Derived from *Money Income and Poverty Status 1985*, table 16; *Estimates of Poverty Including Noncash Benefits 1985*, table 2.

16. U.S. Department of Health and Human Services, Family Support Administration, Office of Family Assistance, "Recipient Characteristics and Financial Circumstances of AFDC Recipients," mimeo, 1983, p. 2; also, table 15.

17. According to Murray, of all men in the Michigan data base ages twenty to sixty-four with a high school education (but no more), less than 1 percent are poor. Even for black females, a high poverty group, only 8.5 percent are poor among those who simply complete high school. See Murray with Laren, "According to Age," pp. 68 and 89.

18. *Estimates of Poverty Including Noncash Benefits 1985*, table 2.

19. U.S. Department of Commerce, Bureau of the Census, *Statistical Abstract of the United States 1986* (Washington, D.C.: U.S. Government Printing Office, 1986), table 25.

20. Bruce Jacobs, "The Elderly: How Do They Fare?" (Paper presented at the Working Seminar on the Family and American Welfare Policy, Washington, D.C., October 11, 1986), mimeo, p. 30. Jacobs later writes: "My own calculations suggest that at least one-fifth of the elderly poor population could be brought out of poverty if they converted their home equity" to annual income (p. 32).

21. About 740,000 of the elderly lived in husband-wife families, 122,000 with other relatives. Another third of a million persons over sixty-five, usually women, headed families of their own, presumably composed of relatives or in-laws, some 180,000 of them containing related children under eighteen. *Characteristics of the Population below the Poverty Level: 1984*, table 11.

22. Ibid.

23. *Estimates of Poverty Including Noncash Benefits 1985*, table 2.

24. In 1984, over $10 billion was disbursed through Supplemental Security Income to over 4 million elderly and disabled individuals. U.S. Social Security Administration, *Social Security Bulletin*.

25. The rest of the poor, unrelated individuals lived with nonrelatives, 8 percent in group quarters, the rest in shared households. *Characteristics of the Population below the Poverty Level: 1984*, table 16; and *Money Income and Poverty Status 1985*, table B.

26. In 1970 there were 15.0 million unrelated individuals in the United States; in 1985, 30.5 million. *Statistical Abstract 1986*, table 54; *Money Income and Poverty Status 1985*, table 20.

27. *Characteristics of the Population below the Poverty Level: 1984*, table 8.

28. "As a group, singles suffer a higher rate of poverty than the elderly— 20.9 percent compared to 14.4 percent in 1984—a reversal of the situation in 1970. . . . The poverty rate is highest among those 18–24, almost a third. . . . In New York State, which makes welfare available for single individuals on the same basis as it does for families, singles are the fastest growing group in the welfare population since 1980." Blanche Bernstein, *Saving a Generation* (New York: Twentieth Century Fund, 1986), p. 11.

29. "In New York City they [singles] are disproportionately represented among the homeless. While detailed data are not available, general information and observation suggest that in this group those in poverty suffer from some degree of physical and mental disability, alcoholism, drug abuse, and other behavior problems (including criminal activity) but they were also hard hit by the recession of 1982–83 and the continuing high rate of unemployment." Bernstein, *Saving a Generation*, p. 11.

30. U.S. Department of Commerce, Bureau of the Census, Population Division, telephone inquiry, January 1986 (estimate is for July 1985).

31. U.S. Department of Commerce, Bureau of the Census, Current Population Reports, Series P-20, No. 409, *School Enrollment: Social and Economic Characteristics of Students, October 1985*, table 6. U.S. Department of Defense, special estimate for December 1986 by Mary Orr, Defense Manpower Data Center.

32. U.S. Department of Labor, Bureau of Labor Statistics, *Employment and Earnings*, January 1986, table 3 in Annual Averages section. U.S. Department of Justice, special estimate for 1985 by Lawrence A. Greenfeld, Bureau of Justice Statistics.

33. *Employment and Earnings*, January 1986, table 834.

34. Ibid., tables 3, 4; U.S. Department of Labor, *Labor Force Statistics Derived from the Current Population Survey*, vol. 1, Bulletin no. 2096, September 1986, tables A–3, A–10.

35. *Marital Status and Living Arrangements: March 1984*, table 1. Telephone conversation with Arlene Saluter, Marriage and Family Branch, U.S. Bureau of the Census, January 1987.

36. Richard B. Freeman and Harry J. Holzer, eds., *The Black Youth Employment Crisis* (Chicago: University of Chicago Press, 1986).

37. Richard B. Freeman, "Cutting Black Youth Unemployment: Create Jobs That Pay as Well as Crime," *New York Times*, July 20, 1986.

38. Sixty percent of black men sixteen to twenty-four had no work experience in 1985. *Employment and Earnings*, January 1986, table 3 in Annual Averages section.

39. Freeman, "Cutting Black Youth Unemployment."

40. Ibid.

41. These included reading, working around the house, going to school, working or looking for work. In comparison, the category "Hanging Out/ Friends/Bars/Parties" accounted for 14.5 percent of the average individual's daily time. Freeman and Holzer, *The Black Youth Employment Crisis*, pp. 355–58.

42. Freeman, "Cutting Black Youth Unemployment."

43. Ibid.

44. Ibid.

45. Ibid. See also Richard B. Freeman, "The Relationship of Churchgoing and Other Background Factors to the Socio-economic Performance of Black Male Youths from Inner-City Tracts," in Freeman and Holzer, eds., *The Black Youth Employment Crisis*.

46. Freeman, "Cutting Black Youth Unemployment." See also Robert I. Lerman, "Who Are the Young Absent Fathers?" *Youth and Society*, September 1986, pp. 3–27.

47. Ibid.

48. Ibid.

49. William Julius Wilson, "The Urban Underclass in Advanced Industrial Society," in Paul E. Peterson, ed., *The New Urban Reality* (Washington, D.C.: Brookings Institution, 1985), p. 133.

50. The total population—of all races—living in poverty tracts in the biggest 100 cities comes to 5.2 million. Nathan, "The Underclass: Will It Always Be with Us?" p. 7. Most of the underclass can be found in an even more narrowly focused field. In the 50 biggest cities, there were 4.4 million persons in poverty tracts. Calculation by Richard Nathan and John Lago, personal correspondence. See also chapter 4, note 1, in this volume. Douglas G. Glasgow writes: "The current size of the black underclass defies precise estimates. Some sources estimate as many as five to seven million persons." Douglas G. Glasgow, "The Black Underclass in Perspective," in Janet Dewart, ed., *The State of Black America 1987* (Washington, D.C.: National Urban League, 1987), p. 131, citing "America's Underclass: Doomed to Fail in the Land of Opportunity," *The Economist*, March 15, 1986, p. 29.

51. Comparing 1970 and 1980 decennial census data for the nation's 50 largest cities, Nathan and Lago found that while these cities as a group lost population (5.1 percent), their poverty population grew by 11.7 percent. The white poverty population of these 50 cities *declined* by 18.3 percent between 1970 and 1980; on the other hand, the black poverty population increased by 18.0 percent. The number of poor blacks in poverty areas rose at an even faster rate—22.6 percent. The number of blacks in extreme poverty areas—

defined as census tracts having 40 percent or more people in poverty—rose by 58.6 percent. Nathan and Lago, personal correspondence.

52. Ken Auletta writes: "Among students of poverty there is little disagreement that a fairly distinct black and white underclass does exist; that this underclass generally feels excluded from society, rejects commonly accepted values, suffers from *behavioral* as well as *income* deficiencies. They don't just tend to be poor; to most Americans their behavior seems aberrant." Ken Auletta, *The Underclass* (New York: Random House, 1982), p. 1 (emphasis in original). See also Glasgow, "The Black Underclass in Perspective."

53. Nathan, "The Underclass," p. 5.

54. Thomas F. Pettigrew, "Social Psychology's Potential Contributions to an Understanding of Poverty," in Vincent T. Covello, ed., *Poverty and Public Policy: An Evaluation of Social Science Research* (Boston: G. K. Hall, n.d.), p. 219.

55. Richard P. Nathan, "The Concentration of Poor People in Poverty Areas in the Nation's 100 Largest Central Cities," tables for presentation to the New School for Social Research, November 14, 1986, p. 1.

56. Ibid., p. 3.

57. Ibid.

58. Glenn C. Loury, "Race and Poverty: The Problem of Dependency in a Pluralistic Society" (Paper presented at the Working Seminar on the Family and American Welfare Policy, Washington, D.C., November 10, 1986), mimeo, p. 4.

3

The Poor Family

As we have already seen, three-fifths of the poor live in families with children under eighteen. Of the 33 million persons below the official poverty line in 1985, the bulk of the poor (25.7 million) lived in families. (A family is defined by the Census Bureau as two or more persons related by marriage, blood, or adoption and living together under the same roof.)

Using the broadest official measure, there were, in all, 7.2 million poor families, and in the "market-valued" measure, 4.7 million (see chapter 2, table 2–1). When public policy helps a family with children out of poverty, it typically helps three or four persons at once, thus multiplying the effect of its assistance both for the current generation and, ideally, the next. In the (broadly taken) 7.2 million poor families of 1985, there were 12.5 million children under eighteen.[1] (Another half-million poor children lived in foster care, on their own [older teens], and in other arrangements.)

Poor white families outnumbered poor black families, approximately 5 million to 2 million. In absolute numbers, family poverty in America is *predominantly* a white problem. But, of course, black families are *disproportionately* poor: a full 29 percent of all black families are poor, compared to 9 percent of white families. Part of the reason for this is that 47 percent of black families are headed by a single parent.[2]

Among all families below the poverty line, just under half are intact husband-wife families (3.44 million), and slightly more are female headed (3.47 million); the rest are headed by single males. But these figures obscure a crucial point. *Of all husband-wife families (about 51 million), only 6.7 percent are below the official poverty line; 93.3 percent are not.* By contrast, of female-headed families, 34 percent are below the government's poverty line[3] (see table 3–1).

Two persons working full time at the minimum wage can earn enough (approximately $13,500) to lift a family of four above the poverty line; a single parent obviously cannot. Of course, if one parent is disabled or at home with small children or unable to maintain full-time employment, not even a two-parent family can do so. But its chances are better.

Since 1969, after having declined somewhat, the number of poor families with children under eighteen has steadily risen. By 1985 families with minor children accounted for 20.5 million of the official poverty population, including the 12.5 million children already mentioned and approximately 8 million caretakers. (There were also about 1.6 million poor families, containing 5.2 million persons, that did not have children under eighteen.)[4]

TABLE 3–1

FAMILIES AND POOR FAMILIES, 1985
(millions)

| | | Poor Families | | Poverty Rate | |
	Number of Families	Cash income only	After noncash benefits[a]	Cash income only	After noncash benefits[a]
All families	63.6	7.2	4.7	11	8
Husband-wife	50.9	3.4	2.4	7	5
Female-headed	10.2	3.5	2.1	34	20
White families					
Husband-wife	45.9	2.8	2.1	6	4
Female-headed	7.1	2.0	1.2	27	17
Black families					
Husband-wife	3.7	.4	.3	12	8
Female-headed	2.9	1.5	.9	51	30
Hispanic families[b]					
Husband-wife	3.0	.5	.4	17	12
Female-headed	1.0	.5	.3	53	29

a. At "market value," excluding institutional expenditures.
b. Persons of Hispanic origin may be of either race, so numbers do not total.

SOURCE: U.S. Bureau of the Census, *Estimates of Poverty Including the Value of Noncash Benefits, 1985*, table 2.

Two-thirds of poor families (4.9 million) have a head under age forty-five. Three quarters (5.6 million) have children under eighteen.[5] Thus, when one says "poor family," one most often (but not always) means two things: (1) young heads of families with (2) children under eighteen.

By sharp contrast, the most economically secure part of the American population consists of those in families without children or older families with grown children eighteen years and over. In 1984, only 4.6 percent of such persons were below the official poverty line. More than 95 percent were not, and their median income was high. As Blanche Bernstein suggests, the reasons for this relative affluence are not hard to discover. Such parents have reached their mature earning power, many wives (relieved of child care responsibilities or never having had them) are working, and grown children are in some cases contributing to family income.[6] It is the families with young children whose incidence of poverty can be expected to be comparatively high.

The Husband-Wife Family

Many single parents succeed in raising children and in keeping their household out of poverty. But, empirically, husband-wife families are more likely to exit from and to stay out of poverty. On the whole, husband-wife families offer greater income-producing and burden-sharing resources. Having both male and female adult role models in the home, and having two sets of connections to the outer world, also seems to benefit children.[7] For such reasons, husband-wife families present fewer problems for public policy while the growing number of female-headed households involves higher public expenditures.

Nonetheless, in 1985, 2.3 million husband-wife families and their 5.4 million children under eighteen lived on incomes below the poverty line. Thus, husband-wife couples with their children constitute 30 percent of the poor.[8] (Another 1.1 million married couples who had no children under eighteen were also poor.) Since the care two persons can offer children—in attention and in guidance—is both priceless and socially indispensable, wise social policy will treasure this model of family life and, at the very least, do it no harm.

Although the nation has few special programs designed specifically to aid husband-wife families among the poor, many qualify for food stamps and other in-kind assistance programs. Moreover, poor husband-wife families will be helped by the doubling to $2,000 (and future indexing) of the exemption for dependents scheduled in the new tax law of 1986. Still, this standard exemption was $600 in 1948; fully corrected for income growth and inflation, it would now reach more than $6,000 per dependent.[9] Further, payroll taxes for social security have become a growing burden, far out of proportion to the taxation imposed upon low-income persons in earlier decades, as Eugene Steuerle has shown.[10]

The empirical difference that husband-wife families make to income is illustrated vividly in census data. In 1985, the median annual income of black female-headed families was $9,305; for black husband-wife families it was $24,570.[11] These sums reflect greater earnings by intact families; in addition, the husband-wife family facilitates both work and career-expanding training, first for one spouse, then another. Family structure makes a powerful difference in annual income and thus in the ability to accumulate net worth. A married couple with children has, on average, $13,600 more in net worth than an otherwise comparable female-headed family with children (1986 dollars).[12]

Yet between 1970 and 1984, as the National Urban League noted in *The State of Black America 1986*, the number of black families headed by women more than doubled (an increase of 113 percent), whereas husband-wife families among blacks grew by only 5 percent.[13] The greater proportion of female-headed families among blacks dramatically lowered average black family income.

Indeed, family structure now plays a far larger role than race in income differentials. In 1967, the income of black two-parent families was only 68 percent of that of two-parent white families; by 1984, this gap had narrowed to 80 percent, and among younger and similarly educated families the gap had almost disappeared.[14]

In 1967, wives contributed 11 percent of white two-parent incomes; in 1984, 18 percent. For black two-parent incomes, the percentages were 19 and 31. Blanche Bernstein comments:

> In general, it takes about 1.3 wage earners per 4-person family to achieve the Bureau of Labor Statistics (BLS) independent but lower-level standard of living ($15,323 in 1981 prices—later figures have not been published for the BLS standards), 1.7 for the moderate level ($24,408), and 2 wage earners for the higher level ($38,060). The female-headed family is clearly at a serious disadvantage.[15]

Thus, even robust economic growth and full employment are not likely to counterbalance the massive changes in family structure the nation has experienced during the past quarter century.

TABLE 3-2

FEMALE HEADS OF FAMILIES BY AGE, 1985
(percent)

Ages	All	Those on AFDC
19–24	8	36
25–34	26	37
35–44	24	18
45 and over	42	8

NOTE: AFDC figures are for 1983, latest available. For AFDC figures, first two age groups are 19–25 and 26–34.

SOURCES: U.S. Bureau of the Census, *Household and Family Characteristics: March 1985*, Series P-20, no. 411, table 9. Dept. of Health and Human Services, *1983 Recipient Characteristics and Financial Circumstances of AFDC Recipients*, table 18.

Female-Headed Families

Originally, Aid to Families with Dependent Children was expected to serve mainly the children of widows. But by 1980, more than half of all AFDC expenditures went to a mother who had had her first child as a teen-ager. These constituted a full 71 percent of all AFDC mothers under the age of thirty.[16]

Among whites, the percentage of female-headed families with children rose from 6 to 15 percent between 1960 and 1985. For blacks the figures went from 21 to 50 percent.[17] A much higher proportion of black women are on AFDC. Still, of all AFDC mothers, 43.3 percent are black; 41.2 percent white.[18]

Between *all* female heads of families (most of whom are not poor) and those on AFDC, there is a significant difference in age distribution (see table 3–2). Two-thirds of all female heads are *older* than thirty-five. Seventy-three percent of AFDC heads are *under* thirty-five (1983), and half are under twenty-five.[19]

Among all female family heads, 55 percent report themselves as divorced or living apart from their husbands; 26 percent are widows; only 18 percent report that they have never married. (There is evidence that the last category is underreported, since some who report themselves as "married, spouse absent" are actually "never married.") Blacks show a higher percentage reporting "never married" (33 percent) and fewer widows (21 percent) (see table 3–3).[20]

47

TABLE 3-3

NUMBER OF FEMALE HEADS OF FAMILIES, 1985
(thousands)

	Total	Widows	Divorced, Separated	Never Married	Poverty Rate
Total	10,129	2,671	5,607	1,850	34.0
White	6,941	1,967	4,150	825	27.4
Black	2,964	627	1,350	989	50.5
Ages 15–24	785	17	269	499	74.2
25–44	5,155	346	3,759	1,052	40.5
45–64	2,736	1,115	1,443	179	21.1
65+	1,454	1,193	139	121	13.3
Median age	41	63	39	29	—

Separated = "married, husband absent."

SOURCES: U.S. Bureau of the Census, *Household and Family Characteristics, March 1985*, table 12; *Money Income and Poverty Status: 1985*, table 19.

Of *poor* female heads of families, 2 million (56 percent) are white; 1.5 million (42 percent) black; and 0.5 million (15 percent) Hispanic. (Numbers do not add because Hispanics can be counted in either race.)[21]

Nearly a half-million births to teen-agers occurred in each recent year. Still, since 1970, the absolute *number* of births to teen-agers has declined, from a high of about 650,000 to just under 500,000. A sharp rise in abortions (and also a decline in the number of teen-agers) helps to account for this. But the *proportion* of out-of-wedlock births to all births has grown, a reflection of declining marriage rates and marital birthrates.[22] Over half of all teen births are now illegitimate.[23]

Census Bureau data show that if the nation had had the same proportion of female-headed households in 1985 as in 1959, there would have been about 5.2 million fewer persons in poverty.[24] A special analysis by the Census Bureau showed that the poverty rate for black families would have been 20 percent in 1980, rather than its actual 29 percent, if black family composition had remained as it was in 1970.[25]

The Children of the Poor

Some 13 million of the U.S. poor (two-fifths) are children under age eighteen. Five million are under age six.[26]

Of all poor families with children, about 15 percent have family heads under age twenty-five. Two-thirds are headed by someone between ages 25 and 44.[27]

Some 5.4 million poor children under eighteen live in a married-couple family. But most—7.1 million (57 percent of those in families) —live with only one parent. Just over a half-million live outside families, in foster care, on their own (older teens), and in other arrangements.[28]

Over half the poor white children live with two parents. Of the 4.1 million poor black children, only 750,000 (18 percent) live with two parents.[29]

There is no escaping the fact that their parents' marital status has consequences for children. Children with two parents benefit by greater adult earnings potential, and those with only one parent are at greater risk, financial and behavioral. This is especially true when the mother receives no child support from the father, has children out of wedlock, has not finished high school, and is unemployed. Blanche Bernstein writes in *Saving a Generation:* "Poverty among some groups —intact families or the elderly—can be reduced by economic measures or by some changes in social insurance programs; among other groups, especially female heads of families and their children, changes in social behavior are essential."[30]

Changes are also needed in programs combating child abuse and neglect, especially with respect to poor families. About 1.7 million children were reported as abused or neglected in 1985, more than eleven times the number in 1963. (About 600,000 of these cases were substantiated.) Increased reporting has helped to reduce deaths from child abuse from nearly 3,000 per year to about 1,000.[31] Unfortunately, recent progress against child abuse has also been accompanied by the misuse of foster care.

In the vast majority of poor families, children are not mistreated but cherished. Still, families reported for mistreatment are four times more likely to be on public assistance. Nearly 85 percent of all substantiated cases involve forms of inadequate child rearing rather than physical danger to the child. Every year, more than 440,000 children spend at least some time in foster care; the vast majority have been in no actual physical danger.

Foster care is supposed to be temporary, but in 1983, 36 percent of the white children and 55 percent of the black children had been in foster care more than two years; some 30 percent of all the children, more than six years. Thus, many children become trapped in a vicious cycle. Since their parents do not show improvement from counseling services, they are not returned home; but since parental rights remain in force, they cannot be placed for adoption, and many live in a kind of emotional limbo. Their physical condition may improve; but their emotional condition frequently deteriorates. As one group of scholars put it, "By its intervention the state may make a bad situation worse: indeed, it may even make a tolerable or even a good situation into a bad one."[32]

In the large majority of cases, in which "child neglect" is actually a sign of social impoverishment, most child care specialists now think it more fruitful to intervene within the family than to remove the children from it. In place of foster care, they urge more child-oriented services that compensate for parental deficiencies. Although less costly than foster care, such compensatory services would not save money, since AFDC and many other welfare payments are suspended when children are placed in foster care. Coalitions of black churches are becoming especially active in offering practical assistance.

In a more general way, the American Public Welfare Association sums up the condition of America's poor children in a recent report, *One Out of Four*:

Economic statistics alone fail to fully illustrate the tragic circumstances of life for poor children and their families.

Child and spousal abuse and neglect are epidemic. Although not limited to poor families, domestic violence is more frequent, more dangerous, and more devastating among families living in poverty.

. . . Ninety-six percent of unmarried teenagers now keep and raise their children, an increase of 11 percent from 1971. The welfare system supports many of these children with children.

Single-parent, female-headed households living in poverty in this country have increased dramatically, from 2.4 million to 3.4 million between 1975 and 1985. Nearly 40 percent of all single-parent, female-headed households live in poverty in 1986. Single-parent households are four times more likely to be poor than are two-parent families.[33]

Neither nature nor the U.S. government nor the U.S. economic system commands children under seventeen to have children, mostly out of wedlock. This is not in accord with the morality we have inherited nor with the nation's past history. In such large numbers, this is a relatively recent development, and understanding how it came about is a crucial matter. Even though its springs lie in personal behavior, the latter in turn may be pulled along by the currents of the reigning social ethos.

In this respect, the U.S. social system has three parts: a political system, an economic system, and a moral system. The major large institutions of the moral system are the universities, schools, religious institutions, and media, especially the organs of popular culture that establish expectations for behavior. As Charles Krauthammer has written:

> Kids do not learn their morals at school. (Which is why the vogue for in-school drug education will prove an expensive failure.) They learn at home. Or they used to. Now they learn from the culture, most notably from the mass media. Your four-eyed biology teacher and your pigeon-toed principal say don't. The Pointer Sisters say do. To whom are you going to listen?
>
> My authority for the fact that teen-age sex-control is an anachronism is Madonna. "Papa don't preach," she sings. "I'm gonna keep my baby." She is months—nine months to be precise—beyond the question of sex. Her mind's already on motherhood.
>
> Kids are immersed in a mass culture that relentlessly says yes. A squeak from the schools saying no, or a tacit signal saying maybe, is not going to make any difference. To pretend otherwise is grossly to misread what shapes popular attitudes. What a school can credibly tell kids depends a lot on whether they grew up on the Pillsbury Doughboy or on a grappling group of half-nudes spaced out on Obsession.[34]

One cannot tackle the problems of poverty among children, especially the problems of teen-age pregnancy and out-of-wedlock birth, without facing the social behaviors taught by popular culture. But we must also face the fact that AFDC is no longer a program mainly for widows. It helps many divorced or separated women to get through a period of temporary need. But it has also become a program that finances increasing numbers of out-of-wedlock births.[35]

No wonder that the chairman of the Senate Subcommittee on Social Security and Family Policy, Senator Daniel Patrick Moynihan, announced at his first hearing in the 100th Congress that it is too late to reform AFDC and proposed replacing it with something entirely different. He called AFDC obsolete, saying that it "grew and grew and grew" until now it supports 7 million children and pays more than $15 billion in benefits a year. Such a program, he continued, "will not be supported in a world where mothers are poor because they are unsupported by their divorced husbands or because they are unwed. A program that was designed to pay mothers to stay at home with their children cannot succeed when we now observe most mothers going out to work."[36] The time seems unusually auspicious for common action.

Notes

1. The other 0.5 million poor children (there were 13 million total) were either living in their own household (sixteen to seventeen-year olds) or with nonrelatives. U.S. Department of Commerce, Bureau of the Census, Current Population Reports, Series P-60, No. 154, *Money Income and Poverty Status of Families and Persons in the United States: 1985 (Advance Data from the March 1986 Current Population Survey)* (Washington, D.C.: U.S. Government Printing Office, 1986), table 16.

2. U.S. Department of Commerce, Bureau of the Census, Technical Paper 56, *Estimates of Poverty Including the Value of Noncash Benefits: 1985* (Washington, D.C.: U.S. Government Printing Office, 1986), table 2.

3. Ibid.

4. *Money Income and Poverty Status 1985*, table 16; *Estimates of Poverty Including Noncash Benefits 1985*, table 2.

5. *Estimates of Poverty Including Noncash Benefits 1985*, table 2.

6. Blanche Bernstein, *Saving a Generation* (New York: Priority Press Publications, 1986), pp. 9–10 and table A.1.

7. The prominent clinician and child development authority Yuri Bronfenbrenner has identified having both a mother and a father in the home as an important aid to healthy child development. Writing jointly with Maureen A. Mahoney, he has summarized the research findings:

> There is some evidence that wives without husbands differ from wives in intact families in their relationships to their children. They place more emphasis on obedience, politeness, and conformity (Tiller, 1959), and are slightly less encouraging of masculine behavior in their sons (Biller, 1969). To control their children, they use more extreme disciplinary practices, ranging from overprotectiveness to harsh power assertive techniques, but are frequently unsuccessful (Hetherington and Durr, 1970).

Yuri Bronfenbrenner and Maureen A. Mahoney, *Influences on Human Development*, 2d ed. (Hinsdale, Ill.: Dryden Press, 1972), p. 421.

8. *Estimates of Poverty Including Noncash Benefits 1985*, table 2.

9. Eugene Steuerle, "The Tax Treatment of Households of Different Size," in Rudolph G. Penner, ed., *Taxing the Family* (Washington, D.C.: American Enterprise Institute, 1983), p. 74. According to other calculations by Steuerle and Paul Wilson, in 1975 a working, four-person family with a poverty level income received a tax *refund* (through the Earned Income Tax Credit) amounting to 4.55 percent of its income. By 1986, that same family had to *pay* income taxes equal to 3.26 percent of its income. Eugene Steuerle and Paul Wilson, "The Taxation of Poor and Lower Income Workers," in Jack A. Meyer, ed., *Ladders Out of Poverty: A Report of the Project on the Welfare of Families*, Bruce Babbitt and Arthur Flemming, co-chairs (Washington, D.C.: American Horizons, 1986), pp. 49–50.

10. In 1986, a working, four-person family at one-half the median income paid 14.3 percent of its income in social security taxes. This compares to 11.7 percent in 1976, 8.4 percent in 1966, and 4.0 percent in 1956. See Steuerle and Wilson, "The Taxation of Poor and Lower Income Workers," table 6. See also part two, chapter 2, note five, above. When both state and federal income taxes as well as payroll taxes (including all social security withholdings) are considered, a working, four-person family at the poverty level is today paying over 19 percent of its earnings in taxes. Welfare recipients, of course, avoid these taxes altogether. On this, see Robert D. Reischauer, "Welfare Reform and the Working Poor" (Paper prepared for inclusion in *Reducing Poverty and Dependency*, forthcoming in 1987 from the Center for National Policy, pp. 12–13).

11. *Money Income and Poverty Status 1985*, table 1.

12. John Weicher and Susan Wachter, "The Distribution of Wealth among Families" (Paper presented to the Working Seminar on the Family and American Welfare Policy, November 10, 1986).

13. National Urban League, *The State of Black America 1986* (Washington, D.C.: National Urban League, 1986).

14. *Money Income and Poverty Status 1985*, table 1; U.S. Department of Labor, Bureau of Labor Statistics, *Handbook of Labor Statistics* (annual).

15. Bernstein, *Saving a Generation*, pp. 7–8.

16. Kristin A. Moore and Martha F. Burt, *Private Crisis, Public Cost: Policy Perspective on Teenage Childbearing* (Washington, D.C.: Urban Institute, 1981).

17. U.S. Department of Commerce, Bureau of the Census, Current Population Reports, Series P-20, no. 411, *Household and Family Characteristics: March 1985* (Washington, D.C.: U.S. Government Printing Office, 1986), table 3, and earlier years.

18. Thirteen percent are Hispanic, 1 percent Native American, 1.5 percent Asian. *1983 AFDC Recipients Study*, p. 1.

19. *Household and Family Characteristics: March 1985*, table 9; and U.S. Department of Health and Human Services, Family Support Administration, Office of Family Assistance, *Recipient Characteristics and Financial Circumstances of AFDC Recipients* (mimeo), 1983, p. 1.

20. *Household and Family Characteristics: March 1985*, table 12.

21. *Money Income and Poverty Status 1985*, table 19.

22. U.S. National Center for Health Statistics, *Vital Statistics of the United States* (annual).

23. Ibid.

24. Calculated using 1985 poverty rates and 1959 family composition from *Money Income and Poverty Status 1985*, table 16. See also Michael Novak, "On Social Invention: Some Reflections on the Relationship between Family and Poverty," *Yale Law and Policy Review*, vol. 4 (Fall/Winter 1985), pp. 88–89.

25. Gordon Green and Edward Welniak, "Changing Family Composition and Income Differentials" (Washington, D.C.: U.S. Department of Commerce, Bureau of the Census, 1982).

26. *Money Income and Poverty Status 1985*, table 18.

27. *Characteristics of the Population below the Poverty Level: 1984*, table 15.

28. *Estimates of Poverty Including Noncash Benefits 1985*, table 2.

29. Ibid.

30. Bernstein, *Saving a Generation*, p. 3.

31. U.S. National Center on Child Abuse and Neglect, *National Analysis of Official Child Abuse and Neglect Reporting (1978)* (Washington, D.C.: U.S. Government Printing Office), p. 36, table 28. This is the last year for which reliable data are available.

32. J. Goldstein, A. Freud, and A. Solnit, *Before the Best Interests of the Child* (New York: Free Press, 1980), p. 13.

33. American Public Welfare Association and the National Council of State Human Service Administrators, *One Child in Four*, p. 9.

34. Charles Krauthammer, "Teen-Age Sex: The Battle Is Lost," *Washington Post*, December 5, 1986.

35. Again, 46 percent of the 7 million children covered by AFDC in 1983 had parents not joined in wedlock. *1983 AFDC Recipients Study*, p. 2; also, table 15.

36. Daniel Patrick Moynihan, "Beyond Welfare," Statement before the Senate Subcommittee on Social Security and Family Policy, January 23, 1987, pp. 5–7.

4

Other Behavioral Dimensions

In addition to the conventional disaggregations of the poor already noted, other behavioral dimensions also shed light on the condition of dependency. Where do the poor live? How do they house themselves? What is their relation to the labor force and to employment? Income aside, what are their actual expenditures? There is, finally, the question of the worst affliction visited on the poor, or at least upon some of them, an affliction far worse than the mere fact of low income: being victimized by crime.

The Geography of the Poor

It may come as a surprise that some 70 percent of the population with incomes below the government poverty line live outside the largest 100 cities.[1] About 10 million live in rural areas, about 9 million in suburban areas, and about 14 million in cities small and large. More of the poor live in the South (12.9 million persons), the largest region, than in the Northeast and the West together (5.8 million and 6.2 million, respectively).[2] Just the same, large urban inner-city areas do contain many of the pathologies associated with the meanest sufferings of the poor, which properly shock the conscience of the nation.

The lower cost of living, lower crime rates, and generally more pleasant surroundings outside the cities make rural poverty appear to be less grinding. Higher wage rates and typically higher benefits, however, have drawn millions of migrants from rural areas to the cities, and greater urban opportunities have over the years helped many to exit from poverty.

We have already noted the special poverty of families headed by women. These, alas, are concentrated where such poverty is worst: almost half of all such poor families (44 percent) live in center cities (see table 4–1). Another million (28 percent) live in rural areas.[3] There, too, and among whites, the new morality—families headed by women, out-of-wedlock pregnancy—seems slowly to be growing, fed by the same popular culture, supported by the same availability of

55

TABLE 4–1

FAMILIES HEADED BY WOMEN, BY RESIDENCE, 1983
(millions)

	Total		Below Poverty Line	
	No.	Percent	No.	Percent
Total	9.9	100	3.6	100
In metropolitan areas	7.2	73	2.5	69
Center cities	3.9	39	1.6	44
Suburbs	3.3	33	.9	25
In rural areas	2.7	27	1.0	28

SOURCE: Census Bureau, *Characteristics of the Population below the Poverty Level: 1983*, Series P-60, no. 147, table 9.

AFDC.[4] Cause and effect are not clear, but the development is clear enough.

Where do poor children live? Most poor white children live either in rural areas (43 percent) or in the suburbs (29 percent), 28 percent in center cities. For blacks these proportions are nearly reversed: 58 percent of poor black children live in center cities, only 28 percent in rural areas, and 14 percent in suburbs.[5] These proportions roughly follow the distributions of the total black and white populations.[6]

Poor white children in rural areas are probably not suffering under the harsh conditions most poor black children meet in urban areas. Although they belong to families whose incomes fall below the poverty line, their condition may seem relatively close to that of many of their nonpoor companions. By contrast, poor black children are concentrated in areas where other hazards may be worse than falling below the official poverty line. To be below the poverty line in rural areas of Utah, Kansas, or Maine may not imply dependency or dysfunction, but below-poverty living in center-city Chicago, Cleveland, or New York often does.

In general, then, white child poverty is predominantly a rural-suburban problem, but the poverty of black children is predominantly an urban problem. Some 2.5 million of the 4.1 million poor black children under eighteen live in central cities. Four fifths of them are living with a single parent, usually their mother.[7]

Geography is one of the defining characteristics of the "underclass," concentrated as we have seen in high-poverty census tracts in center cities. Indeed, 60 percent of all AFDC cases are concentrated in only ten states, each of which contains one or more such urban areas (see appendix).

How Are the Poor Housed?

Of the 7.6 million poor families in 1983, 3.1 million lived in owner-occupied units (41 percent).[8] This is important not only for the sense of independence it engenders but also for affording at least a modest capital asset amid the contingencies of life, and to pass on to the next generation. For the poor as for most other Americans, home ownership constitutes by far the largest portion of net worth. Home ownership is a sign of higher economic status, achieved either through inheritance or through a sufficiently steady income to pay the costs of down payment, mortgage, and property taxes, even though income in some years may fall below the poverty line.

Table 4–2 shows that in 1983 almost as many poor families lived in central cities (35 percent) as in rural areas (39 percent). But 56 percent of the poor who lived in rural areas owned their own homes while only 23 percent in central cities did.[9]

In 1983 not quite 60 percent of poor families were renters. A quarter of these (15 percent all poor families) lived in subsidized or public housing. As might be expected, younger poor families tended to rent. Only by the age of forty-five did heads of poor families who owned their own homes begin to outnumber heads who rented. Accordingly, the median age of all home-owning poor people was forty-eight, and of renters thirty-three.[10]

TABLE 4–2

HOME OWNERSHIP BY THE POOR,
BY AREA OF RESIDENCE, 1983
(percent)

Area of Residence	Poor Families Living in Specified Areas	Poor Owning Homes in Each Area
Total	100	41
In rural areas	39	56
In suburbs	26	42
In center cities	35	23

SOURCE: Census Bureau, *Characteristics of the Population below the Poverty Level: 1983*, Series P-60, no. 147, table 23.

Female heads of families with related children under eighteen are overwhelmingly renters. Twice as many poor families with related children under eighteen rent as own. Many of the families who rent—some 1.8 million whose householder is under sixty-five—have no worker at all earning income.[11]

Some 85 percent of the families in poverty areas in central cities are renters, 41 percent of them in publicly owned or subsidized housing.[12] In large rental units crime, vandalism, and other offensive behavior by just a minority of tenants can turn the home life of others into misery. Rules for acceptable behavior are often absent or are not enforced. Noise, disorder, disrepair, and disrespect for property are often unchecked.

Still, although it appears that low-income rural families have significant advantages in home ownership, a low-cost environment, and safety, dependency can exact its toll even in rural settings. Here lack of jobs and isolation play a far clearer role than in the cities. Henry Caudill described a region in Kentucky for the *Washington Post*:

> "The major health problem in this region is just plain depression. If they could go out and work it would do more for their health than anything that could be done." Entire hollows, he said, of 30 to 40 families are on welfare and food stamps. "As their children grow up, they emulate the people they see growing up . . . . We have a medical condition down here—the Appalachian syndrome, the chronic, passive dependency syndrome, in which people just give up. They don't commit crimes or steal. They just stay home."[13]

Charles Murray and others have reported that dysfunctional behaviors once thought to be chiefly confined to urban settings, including increased rates of illegitimacy and prolonged dependency on welfare, are spreading rapidly to rural areas, too.[14]

Employment and Employability

Some 11 million of the poor (33 percent) are too young (under fifteen) and 3.5 million (11 percent) too old (sixty-five and over) to be in the labor force (see figure 4–1). Only a little over half the poor (56 percent) are adults of working age, and these include the disabled. It is useful to keep these proportions in mind in thinking about the work efforts of the poor.

Still, this image needs to be corrected by another. In the historical human pattern, an adult generation cares for its elderly members and for its children. To carry this burden well, that generation needs the earnings that come from work. But today a significant population of

FIGURE 4–1

Poverty Profile by Age, 1985

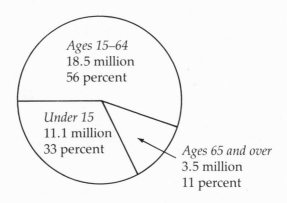

Ages 15–64
18.5 million
56 percent

Under 15
11.1 million
33 percent

Ages 65 and over
3.5 million
11 percent

Source: Census Bureau, *Money Income and Poverty Status: 1985*, table 15.

able, nonelderly adults stay on welfare for more than two years (and sometimes for more than one intermittent spell).[15] Rather than supporting the elderly and the young, they themselves are long-term dependents. For most such persons, a change in family structure is the precipitating cause of dependency but, as Lawrence Mead writes, "the next most important cause is limited working hours."[16] Mead finds that dependents seek work less frequently than others and also work less.

Mead presents a table that demonstrates the dramatic effect of work in reducing poverty (see table 4–3). For families with even one worker, poverty rates are cut in half. With two workers, this half is again substantially reduced. For example, the poverty rate for black families with no workers, is 69 percent; with one worker, 35 percent; with two workers, 8 percent. Clearly, work is an effective path out of poverty, and the number of workers per family matters a great deal.

Like others, nearly all the poor depend for income—and that means work—on their heads of household. Using 1984 figures, Peter Gottschalk and Sheldon Danziger argue, however, that just over half the 14 million heads of poor households should be thought of as "not expected to work."[17] By this they mean those over sixty-five, or disabled, or full-time students, or women with a child under six. Of the half who *are* expected to work, they report, roughly equal numbers did not work at all, worked a full year, and worked part of

TABLE 4-3

POVERTY RATE FOR ALL FAMILIES
AND FEMALE-HEADED FAMILIES,
BY SELECTED EMPLOYMENT CHARACTERISTICS AND RACE, 1985
(percent)

	All Races	White	Black	Hispanic
All families				
Total	11.4	9.1	28.7	25.5
Number of workers				
None	30.1	23.0	68.9	71.8
One	16.0	12.9	34.9	30.5
Two	4.6	4.2	8.3	10.8
Three or more	3.2	2.6	8.3	6.9
Female-headed families				
Total	34.0	27.4	50.5	53.1
Number of workers				
None	72.8	64.8	86.6	90.2
One	30.5	24.8	44.9	43.8
Two	10.9	8.3	20.8	16.9
Three or more	7.7	4.9	15.1	6.2

SOURCE: U.S. Bureau of the Census, *Money Income and Poverty Status of Families and Persons in the United States: 1985*, table 19.

the year—although in the last two categories the hours worked per week were not always full time (see table 4–4).

Gottschalk and Danziger conclude that "workfare" or "job creation" strategies would affect barely more than half the poor. If targeted mainly on those who do not work at all, such strategies would affect only 15 percent of poor heads of households (and, of course, their dependents); and if part-time workers were included, another 15 percent. In their view just over half the households of the poor are beyond the reach of job creation and workfare.

Except for the elderly, however, the Gottschalk-Danziger definition of "not expected to work" is very loose. They are correct that among the poor are many students, disabled persons, and mothers with children under six; and they suggest that persons in such categories are normally "not expected to work." Among the nonpoor, however, many full-time students *do* work (at least part time and during

60

TABLE 4-4

Work Experience of Poor Heads of Households, 1984

	Number (millions)	Percent
Total	14.1	100
"Not expected to work"	7.5	53
Worked 49 weeks or more	2.1	15
Worked 48 weeks or less	2.4	17
Did not work at all	2.1	15

SOURCE: Danziger and Gottschalk, "Poverty and the Underclass."

vacations), many disabled persons work, and many mothers with children under six work. Shouldn't the poor "be expected to work" at least at the levels of the nonpoor?

Moreover, Census Bureau surveys in 1985 found that only 1.3 million (13 percent) of the poor ages fifteen to sixty-four reported that they did not work during the year because they were "unable to find work." Of those poor who worked only part of the year, 60 percent cited factors other than inability to find a job as their reason for not working full time. A shortage of employment opportunities is not reported by the poor as the major reason for not working.[18]

Failure to work, in any case, is clearly a major cause of poverty. In 1984 among all poor mothers of children under eighteen, for example, only 9 percent worked full time for at least forty weeks; another 30 percent worked either fewer weeks or only part time. Among those with children older than six, only 12 percent worked full time for at least forty weeks.[19] In brief, employment rates for poor mothers with children under eighteen are significantly lower than for nonpoor mothers with children.[20] In general, poor mothers are less often employed, and many also suffer from the absence of another adult earner.

Labor-force participation rates (that is, rates of working or seeking employment) are clearly lower among the poor than among the nonpoor. This is particularly striking both among young males and among young female heads of families. It is considerably more true of blacks than of whites.[21]

Lawrence Mead points out that the reasons offered in earlier years for less work by the poor have lost much of their force: that jobs are not available, or are "mismatched" to the skills of the poor, or are geographically "inaccessible," or cannot be taken until more childcare

61

is available. These are not reasons given by most of the poor, and researchers have been unable to find much evidence to support them.[22]

Mead also points out that the traditional image of unemployment —the sole breadwinner thrown out of work—is valid for considerably less than half of today's unemployed. More than half of job seekers left their earlier jobs voluntarily or are just coming into the labor force (for the first time or after an absence). About a third of workers today are workers from families in which someone else is also working.[23] Most of the unemployed are not so for long; half have been unemployed for seven weeks or less.[24] The American tendency to move in and out of jobs is high, a sign of confidence in job prospects; accordingly, the major part of today's unemployment is due to turnover, not lack of jobs. The economy has seldom produced more jobs faster than during the past fifteen years. Never has so high a proportion of adults ages sixteen and over been employed.[25] And in only two decades in the past has a larger stream of immigrants entered the country, mostly to claim jobs at lower entry-level positions.

Employment is always concrete and local, in the sense that a person seeking a job must be matched with a specific employer. Thus even though, nationally, low-skill entry jobs may be available, certain local communities or urban centers may have been so hard hit by severe unemployment that far fewer jobs at all levels are available than elsewhere. Mead's work shows that one may not licitly generalize from such areas to the nation as a whole, and that arguments made from national data may not apply in specific geographical areas.

Mead argues that in most places jobs are in general not *unavailable* to nonworkers but *unacceptable* to them, because of low wages or unpleasant conditions. "Working welfare mothers and low-income black youths themselves say they usually can find minimum-wage jobs fairly easily," he writes.[26] Moreover, the fastest-growing occupations for the foreseeable future, he continues, are and will be relatively low skilled—hospital workers, maintenance workers, cashiers, waiters, hotel workers. "To get *some* job today, workers usually need offer employers no more than literacy, obedience, and the ability to get to work on time."[27] The alleged mismatch of location between job seekers in the city and jobs in the suburbs fails inspection.[28] As for child care, most working mothers, poor or not poor, arrange care informally through relatives, friends, or neighbors.[29]

For about two decades, the work effort of the poor has declined. Until recently, little in the welfare system insisted that recipients had an obligation to work. Such requirements as there were proved easy to take lightly (by seeking work in a purely formal way, for example, without really seeking it). Meanwhile, the out-migration from high-poverty areas of persons who did work for a living often left behind an increasingly large proportion of able adults who did *not* work, and a pattern of nonwork took hold.

The recent report of the American Public Welfare Association attacks this problem head-on, with an eloquent statement on community and self-reliance.

> Family self-sufficiency depends on employment. Unless you are prepared to say—and we are not—that single parents shall always be dependent on welfare, our policies should encourage parents to be qualified to enter the work force, and to take part in the community around them.

> Children do not benefit, in the long run, from having the single parent at home fulltime if they do not also learn about self-sufficiency and the options available to them in the larger community. *Self-responsibility and community involvement are more readily apparent to a child if the parent sets such an example.* In all the rhetoric about self-sufficiency and an end to welfare dependency, we too often forget that the routine of job seeking and job retention are not routine in some families because no family member has ever held a job. Maintaining connections to the community, even when the children are infants, is desirable because it radically reduces the isolation of poor young mothers and heightens opportunities for single parents to work and gain self-sufficiency (italics added).[30]

The public climate has changed and the national ethos is regaining its vigor; thus the prognosis for a resurgence of the work ethic is better than it has been for some time. *Fortune* magazine anticipates that by the end of the 1990s the United States will have created 13 million new jobs and, given the smaller cohort of workers coming along after the "baby boom," severe labor shortages are likely to appear.[31] The time for replacing dependency with patterns of work is opportune. Most welfare recipients who have been obliged to work as a condition for receiving benefits report being happy to work.[32] Work satisfies human longings for social belonging, independence, achievement, and responsibility. It is a mistake to overlook its profound psychological importance, precisely for persons already suffering from low self-esteem. Work not only cuts poverty rates quite sharply; it also quite sharply raises morale.

More Resources Than Meet the Eye

Even without reporting employment, the poor report annual expenditures that exceed their reported annual income. We can gain consid-

63

erable insight into their actual preferences—and their condition—by studying these reported expenditures.[33]

Common sense leads us to expect that reasoning people, aware of the hazards and contingencies of life, will normally husband resources to have them available for expenditure during periods when their income is low. For example, one family out of work for three months during one year may suffer a sharp decline in annual income but keep its expenditures constant by drawing down assets. Another family may ride out periods of low income without lowering its expenditures through the use of government transfers. And a third family may show a pattern of annual expenditures significantly larger than its reported income through drawing on the underground economy, the dimensions of which may be quite large.[34]

Such considerations may help to explain the findings of the latest comprehensive government survey of household expenditures (made in 1984), which showed that the expenditures of the lowest 40 percent of income earners substantially exceeded their reported pretax income. *For the poorest 20 percent total expenditures were actually over three times as great as pretax income.*[35]

Furthermore, through their actual patterns of expenditure, the poor express their own perceptions of need in ways quite different from the expectations of the official definition of poverty. That definition assumes that poor families and households will, on the average, devote one-third of their expenditures to food.[36] In 1984, however, the poorest fifth of all urban households devoted only 19 percent of their expenditures to food. For households headed by persons under twenty-five years of age and with an income under $5,000 per year (households by the official definition clearly in poverty), 21 percent of expenditures were devoted to food. In households headed by a person over sixty-five and with a total money income of less than $5,000, the fraction allocated to food was less than 20 percent. No identified group in the United States today allocates a third of its expenditures for food (see table 4–5).

Nor can it be maintained that, on the average, the diet of the poor is deficient in caloric intake. Food consumption by the poor is not widely discrepant in nutrient value from that of the not poor (see appendix). Some of the poor, however, do not avail themselves of nutritional values well within their reach, less because of low income than because of habit. Anecdotally, an account of the diet of poor children in Appalachia makes this point:

> [Henry Caudill] says the government food programs for women, infants and children give out nutritious foods such

TABLE 4–5

Food expenditures as a Percentage of Total Expenditures for Selected Urban Households, 1980–1981 to 1984

	1980–1981	1982–1983	1984
Black households	20.6	17.9	17.5
White and other households	18.6	16.5	15.4
Householder under 25, income less than $5,000	22.4	20.9	n.a.
Householder over 65, income less than $5,000	24.3	19.3	n.a.

n.a. = not available.
SOURCES: Bureau of Labor Statistics, *Consumer Expenditure Survey: Interview Survey, 1980/81; idem, Consumer Expenditure Survey: Interview Survey, 1982/83* (Washington, D.C.: Department of Labor, February 1986); and idem, *Consumer Expenditure Survey: Interview Survey, 1984.*

as cheese to tradition-bound people who simply won't eat it. "They want beans, corn bread and pork. Things they are accustomed to. You have people who are poorly nourished who drink three or four Cokes a day. A large problem is not the availability of food but the knowledge of how to use it." He said people who work in grade school cafeterias tell him they throw away half the lunch food. "That's because the menus call for things the children aren't accustomed to."[37]

This anecdote shows that there are ranges both of provident and of improvident behavior among the poor, as well as among the affluent. It suggests, too, that the diets of Americans vary widely by ethnicity and custom. Finally, it dramatizes how choice is today of higher significance than ever before. This bears out the general point of this section, that expenditures, for food among other things, may tell us more than income figures do—and things that income figures by themselves cannot.

Crime

The civil right of the poor most often violated today is their right to the integrity of life, limb, and property. Of all the sufferings of the poor, those from crime may be the most oppressive. In census tracts of high-density poverty in inner cities, a significant percentage of the

TABLE 4–6

BURGLARIES, BY HOUSEHOLD INCOME, 1983
(percent)

Income	Households Burglarized in Year
$25,000+	6
$15,000–24,999	7
$10,000–14,999	7
$ 7,500–9,999	7
$ 3,000–7,499	9
Under $3,000	12

SOURCE: Bureau of Justice Statistics, *Criminal Victimization in the U.S.*, 1983.

population falls victim to some crime every year. Over a lifetime the chances are that almost everyone is a victim more than once. High rates of drug abuse, murder, rape, robbery, larceny, and burglary demonstrate flagrant disregard for the humanity of others. Disproportionately, these crimes are committed by young black males.

To have an involuntarily low income is not good; to lack public protection of one's basic right to safety is considerably worse. That the protection of this right is now ineffective is clear enough.

- Only 20 percent of reported crimes are ever solved.
- Among households with annual incomes under $7,500, only 40 percent of burglaries and fewer than one-third of all household crimes are even reported.
- Fewer than 30 percent of those *convicted* of crimes of violence against persons or serious property crimes are sentenced to prison. Just over 70 percent are sent back into the community on "felony probation."
- Some 65 percent of those on felony probation are re-arrested for similar crimes within three years.
- Twice as high a proportion of households of the very poor are burglarized each year as of the affluent.[38]

Table 4–6 is particularly heart-rending. Low-income households have far fewer valuable goods and are far less able to absorb losses. Personal property is about all the capital the poor possess. They often cannot even obtain (if they can afford) property insurance. Hence, as James K. Stewart puts it, "The theft of a TV, furniture, or car can be devastating. Robberies of cash or checks—for rent, welfare, or Social

Security—may at one stroke eliminate a family's ability to pay for home, food, or future."[39]

Personal violence in urban poverty areas adds to low income an environment of terror. The leading cause of death for black males ages 15 to 24 is homicide. Some 1,700 are murdered every year. Around them is an arena of muggings, beatings, rapes, and robberies.[40]

The costs of crime to the poor are not only direct, in financial loss and personal terror, but also indirect. Traditional means by which the poor have advanced themselves—overtime, moonlighting, night school—must often be forgone.

> Why risk a late job or night school if the return home means waiting at deserted bus stops? . . . A secretary declines overtime activities if they extend into the evening . . . . A husband gives up night school rather than leave his wife and young children at home.[41]

Crime lowers property values, making it harder for the urban poor to accumulate capital and to borrow money. Crime is one of the major reasons why businesses in central cities restrict operations, relocate, sell, or close down. The influence of crime on investment decisions is greater than the influence of high taxes or labor costs. Businesses in high-crime areas face sharply higher operating costs, including higher labor costs and investments in a security force, improved lighting, alarms, metal grills for windows and doors, and (if it is available at all) extremely expensive insurance. Such costs are often the difference between survival and failure.

In addition, many good employees and talented managers may refuse employment in crime areas, suppliers may refuse delivery, and customers may be frightened away.

> Neighborhood deterioration usually starts with an increased sense of fear and vulnerability. Commerce slows; people go elsewhere to shop and stay off the streets in the evening; stores put in alarms and bars in the windows; going-out-of-business sales increase, and as businesses change hands, the quality of merchandise declines and prices rise. Buildings get shabbier and some are abandoned. Disorderly street behavior increases. Investments and loans dry up. People who can afford to move out of the area do; schools deteriorate; and the whole community slides down the spiral of economic and social decline.[42]

Life in a high-crime environment is a torment far beyond the difficulties imposed by low income. Reducing crime in poor neighborhoods would remove a scourge. It would lift a heavy and oppressive weight from the shoulders of the poor, freeing many energies for productive and creative self-advancement. It would raise morale. It would reflect respect for basic human dignity.

Notes

1. According to the 1980 census, 31 percent of the poor lived in the nation's 100 largest central cities, 26 percent in the largest 50 cities, and 19 percent in the largest 20. See U.S. Department of Commerce, Bureau of the Census, *U.S. Census of Population 1980: Subject Reports: Poverty Areas in Large Cities* (Washington, D.C., 1985), table 1.

2. U.S. Department of Commerce, Bureau of the Census, Current Population Reports, Series P-60, number 154, *Money Income and Poverty Status of Families and Persons in the United States: 1985 (Advance Data from the March 1986 Current Population Survey)* (Washington, D.C., 1986), table 18.

3. *Characteristics of the Population below the Poverty Level: 1983*, table 9.

4. See Charles Murray, "White Trash," *National Review*, March 28, 1986.

5. *Characteristics of the Population below the Poverty Level: 1983*, table 9.

6. The geographical distribution of children from all income groups is as follows: in center cities: 22 percent of white children, 54 percent of blacks; in suburbs: 43 percent of white children, 21 percent of blacks; in rural areas: 36 percent of white children, 25 percent of blacks. See ibid.

7. Ibid.

8. Ibid., table 23.

9. Ibid.

10. Ibid.

11. Ibid.

12. Ibid.

13. Interview with Judy Mann, *Washington Post*, November 6, 1985.

14. See Murray, "White Trash." See also Lowell Gallaway and Richard Vedder, *The "New" Poverty: Consequences of Past Policy* (Chicago: Heartland Institute, 1986).

15. Fewer than half the women who go onto AFDC are off within two years. Of those who remain into the third year, 60 percent will be on at least six years. See Mary Jo Bane and David Ellwood, "The Dynamics of Dependence: The Routes to Self-Sufficiency" (Prepared for the assistant secretary for planning and evaluation, Department of Health and Human Services, June 1983, mimeo).

16. Lawrence Mead, "The Work Problem in Welfare" (Paper presented at the Working Seminar on the Family and American Welfare Policy, Washington, D.C., October 11, 1986), p. 1, mimeo.

17. Sheldon Danziger and Peter Gottschalk, "Poverty and the Underclass" (Testimony before the House Select Committee on Hunger, August 5, 1986).

18. Other explanations given by the working-age poor as their main reason for not working: ill or disabled, 19 percent; keeping house, 36 percent; going

to school, 23 percent; retired, 4 percent; other, 4 percent. Derived from *Money Income and Poverty Status 1985*, table 18; and *Characteristics of the Population below the Poverty Level: 1984*, table 10. See also Mead, "Work Problem in Welfare," pp. 3–4.

19. *Characteristics of the Population below the Poverty Level: 1984*, table 21.

20. Seventy-three percent of nonpoor mothers with children under eighteen worked, full or part time, for some period in 1984, while 40 percent full time for forty weeks or more. In contrast, 39 percent of poor mothers worked some; only 9 percent worked full time most of the year. Ibid.

21. See Lawrence Mead, "Work and Dependency Part I: The Problem and Its Causes" (Paper written for the Welfare Dependency Project of the Hudson Institute, September 1986, mimeographed), p. 4. Some part of the gap in work effort between the poor and the nonpoor may also be illusory—a function of the movement of some poor into unreported or underground work. See note 34.

22. See Mead, "Work and Dependency, Part I," pp. 8–30; *Money Income and Poverty Status 1985*, table 18; and *Characteristics of the Population below the Poverty Level: 1984*, table 10.

23. Mead, "Work Problem in Welfare," p. 3.

24. U.S. Department of Labor, Bureau of Labor Statistics, *Monthly Labor Review* (December 1986), table 10.

25. The total number of jobs in the country has gone from 79 million in 1970 to 110 million in 1986—a 40 percent increase in sixteen years. The labor force participation rate rose from 60 percent to 66 percent of all adults over the same period. In the past two decades, the number of persons earning a paycheck has increased twice as fast as the population. See *Handbook of Labor Statistics*, and U.S. Department of Labor, Bureau of Labor Statistics, "The Employment Situation" (monthly).

26. See Joel F. Handler and Ellen Jane Hollingsworth, *The "Deserving Poor": A Study of Welfare Administration* (New York: Academic Press, 1971), p. 182; and Richard B. Freeman and Harry J. Holzer, "Young Blacks and Jobs: What We Now Know," *The Public Interest* (Winter 1985), p. 27.

27. Mead, "Work Problem in Welfare," pp. 4–7.

28. David T. Ellwood, "The Spatial Mismatch Hypothesis: Are There Teenage Jobs Missing in the Ghetto?" in Richard B. Freeman and Harry J. Holzer, eds., *The Black Youth Employment Crisis* (Chicago: University of Chicago Press, 1986), chap. 4.

29. Mead, "Work Problem in Welfare," pp. 7–8.

30. American Public Welfare Association, "Family Investment Plan: Questions and Answers," December 1986, mimeographed.

31. *Fortune*, February 2, 1987.

32. Mead, "Work Problem in Welfare," p. 21: "Recipients themselves accept the work test. Strong majorities regard the requirement as just, and most feel positively about their work experience." The evidence that most welfare recipients accept work requirements is summarized in Judith M. Gueron, *Work Initiatives for Welfare Recipients* (New York: Manpower Demonstration Research Corporation, 1986), pp. 13–14.

33. See U.S. Department of Labor, Bureau of Labor Statistics, *Consumer Expenditure Survey: 1984*, August 1986.

34. Some studies suggest that the underground economy now comprises 10-15 percent of GNP. For an informal discussion see Ben J. Wattenberg, *The Good News Is the Bad News Is Wrong* (New York: Simon and Schuster, 1984), pp. 142–45. As regards the poor more specifically, one close analysis of the Michigan longitudinal study of women who were on AFDC in the 1970s shows that 24 percent of the black women still on AFDC in 1980 were earning more than $6,000. To earn more than $6,000 and still receive substantial payments from AFDC requires some explanation. Possibly, some women had large numbers of dependent children; more likely, women were working without reporting it to the welfare office. See Charles Murray with Deborah Laren, "According to Age: Longitudinal Profiles of AFDC Recipients and the Poor by Age Group" (Paper presented at the Working Seminar on the Family and Welfare Policy, Washington, D.C., September 23, 1986, mimeo), p. 55.

35. The 1984 survey by the Bureau of Labor Statistics, based on complete income figures submitted by several thousand nationally representative households, shows that the poorest 20 percent of households had average reported annual income before taxes of $3,200 and annual expenditures of $10,800. U.S. Department of Labor, Bureau of Labor Statistics, *1984 Consumer Expenditure Survey* (pamphlet).

36. The index is based on the Department of Agriculture's 1961 Economy Food Plan and reflects the different consumption requirements of families based on their size and composition. It was determined from the Department of Agriculture's 1955 Survey of Food Consumption that families of three or more persons spend approximately one-third of their income on food; the poverty level for these families was, therefore, set at three times the cost of the Economy Food Plan. For smaller families and persons living alone, the cost of the Economy Food Plan was multiplied by factors that were slightly higher in order to compensate for the relatively larger fixed expenses of these smaller households. The poverty thresholds are updated every year to reflect changes in the Consumer Price Index.

37. Interview with Judy Mann, *Washington Post*.

38. James K. Stewart, "The Urban Strangler," *Policy Review* (Summer 1986), p. 8.

39 Ibid., p. 6.

40. U.S. National Center for Health Statistics, *Vital Statistics* (annual).

41. Stewart, "The Urban Strangler," p. 6.

42. Ibid., p. 8.

5

What Do These Findings Mean?

Reflecting on the Evidence

This long exercise in disaggregating the poor has many practical benefits. First, it demonstrates that, by far, most of the poor live in families—four-fifths in families, three-fifths in families with children under eighteen. It suggests that the 3.5 million elderly poor could be removed from the poverty rolls by the careful execution of programs already in place and by adjustments to cover new realities such as the "elderly-elderly" (or "the frail elderly," as they are sometimes called). It has helped us call attention to the relatively small number—but growing proportions—of the young singles under age thirty-five among poor "unrelated individuals."

We were also able to see that the 3.1 million female-headed families with their 6.7 million children under eighteen constitute almost as many of the poor as married-couple families (2.3 million couples with 5.4 million children)—about 10 million each. But there is one major difference: each of the married-couple families has, as a potential or actual income earner, an additional adult. Then, too, the larger number of female-headed families includes a larger number of children, some 54 percent of all children in families below the poverty line.

Moreover, in paying attention to the young black male, we were able to see that most are performing admirably but that significant numbers, living mainly in high-density poverty tracts in central cities, are not meeting their obligations to themselves or to the common-weal. The geographical concentration of such young males drew our attention to the condition of the so-called underclass of some 4.1 million poor blacks and Hispanics in the same high-density poverty tracts. There, we found, dwell almost half the poor black children, a large majority of whom have in recent years been born out of wed-lock, and in addition, almost half the poor black female heads of households, few of whom were employed full time, year round. In such locations, in particular, but by no means solely in such locations,

71

the new dependency is especially vivid.

Female-headed households and nonwork, we learned, contribute heavily to the low income of the poor. In a sense, low income is far from being the greatest disadvantage they endure. Worse than to live on a low income is to lack the pride that comes from work and self-reliance and the sense of participating in the common tasks of a local and a national community. Internally, some of the adult poor suffer from a lack of preparation for active employment and its necessary disciplines, aptitudes, and attitudes. Externally, many suffer from the threats or actual depradations of criminals who prey most upon those who can afford losses least.

For the elderly, national policy has long since determined that none ought to live in poverty; all should live in decent circumstances.

For able singles, wages from full-time work even at the minimum wage would bring them to a decent standard of living. Finding such work depends in part on an open and growing economy and in part on themselves.

Most poor married-couple families and their children can attain a decent standard of living if both parents work full time at the minimum wage or higher. For married-couple families, a growing economy and rising wage rates would suffice to set the stage for their exit from poverty.

But with regard to poor female-headed families, a growing economy alone is not likely to be enough. One income earner alone cannot support children unless her job pays considerably more than the minimum wage. So how can the number of female-headed families be reduced? Some 46 percent of the children of AFDC mothers were born out of wedlock; the parents of another 20 percent had separated informally. If such numbers are to decrease in the future, so that the lot of newborn children will be more hopeful, both a change in social behavior and parental assumption of responsibility are necessary.

Both absent fathers and AFDC mothers would benefit by having full-time work, year round, even at the minimum wage. Their pride and dignity would be helped, even if their financial situation were little better than with welfare alone. The rising tide of support for work and other obligations on the part of recipients may lead to a public change of signals, incentives, and reinforcement of obligations. If so, current self-damaging trends in family life may be reversed. If not, the national picture may become more bleak.

At the heart of the poverty problem in 1987 is, then, the problem of behavioral dependency. Thus, the public must become quite clear about behaviors it applauds and behaviors it rejects. Major institutions must weigh the signals that they have been sending out. The

poor suffer most from their own dependency; those who unintention-
ally set the stage for it must now help to free them from it. So long as
dependency continues, something in our common life is going wrong
—and we must right it. What do such findings imply? Where do we go
from here? To these questions we turn next, first with reflections, then
with recommendations.

Some Lessons Learned

Twenty-five years ago, as we have seen, President Kennedy without
hesitation stressed "the integrity and preservation of the family unit."
He affirmed that public policy "must contribute to the attack on
dependency . . . family breakdown, illegitimacy."[1] Commending the
president, the *New York Times* editorialized the next day: "No lasting
solution can be bought with a welfare check. The initial cost will
actually be higher than the mere continuation of handouts. The
dividends will come in the restoration of individual dignity and in the
long-term reduction of the need for government help."[2]

These high hopes have not been borne out by the experience of
the American family since 1962. But something important has been
learned. In the first era of the War on Poverty, it was widely thought
that two simultaneous efforts would be sufficient to defeat poverty:
first, sustained economic growth ("a rising tide lifts all boats") and,
second, opening up the social system to opportunity for all, chiefly
through the heroic achievements of the Civil Rights movement. As we
have seen, the prosperity of the past twenty-five years has raised the
condition of the poor in many often overlooked ways: in health,
education, income, housing space per person, the list of "necessary"
household appliances, and the like. The Civil Rights movement de-
monstrably improved the civil, political, and economic status of minorities. Still, the condition of some of the poor— female-headed
families and the underclass—seems to be less hopeful than it was
before. If for such groups economic growth alone is not the answer
and if the opportunity afforded by the dramatic achievements of the
generation since the 1960s is not the answer, what is?

An unwillingness of able adults who receive benefits to work
steadily when work is available would not seem right to those who
believe that citizenship entails duties as well as benefits. There is
evidence for the belief that most poor persons would prefer work and
independence to idleness and dependency. But "prefer" to work is a
long distance from actually working.

Those who have children incur an obligation to work in order to
support their children. This duty is not solely to their children, but

73

also to themselves. It is also a duty toward society at large, the duty of a citizen capable of independence.

Yet during the years 1960–1972, when unemployment rates were dropping from 6 to 3 percent, large increases in single-parent households, teen-age pregnancies, and welfare caseloads occurred.[3] During the 1970s and 1980s, large numbers of immigrants (larger than in any except two previous decades in our history) were attracted to the United States by the broad availability of entry-level jobs and business opportunities. Further, the much-discussed transition to a service economy has generated a broad array of entry-level, low-skilled jobs. Yet during the past two decades black male labor force participation rates have been going *down* and unemployment rates *up*.

Researchers have also learned that youngsters from single-parent households who are on welfare and living in public housing are considerably less likely to complete high school; to learn reading, writing, and arithmetic; to develop skills that would make them employable; to form families; to remain employed; and to support the children they have. With higher frequency than others, they turn to "hustling" and crime and out-of-wedlock children. They are more often financially dependent on others, very often on the government.

There is not sufficient evidence that welfare *causes* these dysfunctions. But there is overwhelming evidence that welfare as now constituted does not offer remedies. Thus, we are obliged to conclude that under current conditions: (1) economic growth is not enough; (2) opportunity is not enough; and (3) welfare as now constituted is not enough.

That is why social inventiveness is needed, if these vulnerable and needy ones are to be helped. In the circumstances, "being helped" means being taught the full range of competences necessary for fulfilling their duties to themselves, to their loved ones, and to their fellow citizens. The elements necessary for attacking dependency have emerged from lessons learned the hard way.

More Evidence of Consensus: In the States and in Four Welfare Reports

Our Working Seminar has had the advantage of studying four other major reports on welfare reform issued late in 1986:

- *Investing in Poor Families and Their Children: A Matter of Commitment*, issued by the American Public Welfare Association and the National Council of State Human Service Administrators
- *Ladders Out of Poverty*, a report of the Project on the Welfare of Families, under the cochairmanship of Governor Bruce Babbitt of

74

Arizona and Arthur Flemming
- *A New Social Contract: Rethinking the Nature and Purpose of Public Assistance*, a report of the Task Force on Poverty and Welfare submitted to Governor Mario M. Cuomo of New York
- *Up from Dependency: A New National Public Assistance Strategy*, issued by the White House Domestic Policy Council, Low Income Opportunity Working Group

These four reports reinforce the original conviction of our Working Seminar that a powerful new consensus has taken shape. In the general thrust of all four reports we find rather astonishing overlaps. All take pains to disaggregate the poor. All praise successes achieved during the past twenty-five years, and all confront the same evidence of serious deterioration among particular populations. All give central importance to the family. All focus upon dependency as a new and primary concern. All stress that benefits to the able must be correlated with obligations to work. All aim at strengthening personal responsibility, self-reliance, and independence. All distinguish between AFDC as a temporary source of support and AFDC as a form of long-term dependency. All encourage the federal government to allow greater flexibility for experimentation by states and localities.

There does not seem to be great disparity in the way these four reports describe the basic data or in the way in which they analyze existing problems or even in most of the general principles that they set forth for dealing with them. There are substantial overlaps even among the programmatic recommendations they make.

Naturally, each report sets forth distinctive proposals that the others ignore or reject (see table 5–1). Each employs some concepts or devises some strategies that are unique. Beneath the surface, each represents a different political agenda and a different practical approach. These differences, of course, are the stuff of politics and of great contestation. Nonetheless, overall, we have been amazed by the breadth and depth of the consensus among these four reports. Concerning particulars, of course, there remains plenty of room for argument. Still, moderation is the mode, incrementalism is the method, and modesty in promises is the tone of all four reports.

Perhaps the single largest difference in these reports concerns their diverse expectations of the federal government. This difference should not be exaggerated.[4] All four reports want more flexibility for state and local governments. All see a vast array of fresh energies, experiments, and new ideas springing up in local contexts.

Moreover, none of the four recommends cuts in the annual levels of funding supplied by the federal government for welfare strategies.

TABLE 5-1
BRIEF COMPARISON OF FOUR REPORTS

	APWA	Babbitt	Cuomo	White House
Summary goals and principles	Investment in children is the key. Each citizen is responsible for self-sufficiency. When poor prosper, we all prosper.	Critical interests: to strengthen the family, to enhance self-sufficiency, and to reduce poverty.	Welfare spending must be viewed as investment in the future productivity of the nation. Stresses reciprocal obligations.	We don't know enough about how to reverse dependency. Experiment widely at local level. Start a *process* of reform, not a program of reform.
Economic growth	Not specifically mentioned.	Not specifically mentioned.	Macroeconomic policies encouraging growth essential. Likewise productive growth may depend on breaking up underclass.	Best antipoverty program in long run. Must foster enterprise. Still, 8 million jobs since 1982 not enough. More than growth needed. Coming labor shortage should help poor.
Tax relief	Make the Earned Income Tax Credit (EITC) vary by family size	Expand the EITC, make variable by family size, index to ratio of median family income. Partial social security tax relief for poor.	Make EITC variable by family size. No poor household should have to pay state or local income tax.	Removal of poor from tax rolls in 1987 one of biggest assists to them in the 1980s. (Family report recommends adjusting EITC for family size.)
Federalism	State levels of need should vary according to local conditions. States should be given	Give states administrative flexibility. Mandate state benefit level minimums. Expand	Tacitly accepts state pre-eminence. Calls for state experimentation. More federal funding, grants,	Maximum flexibility to states. Encourage widespread experiments. Retain current funding.

	administrative flexibility. More federal funding.	federal funding. States pick up other costs as trade.	mandated benefit minimums.	Some "cashing out." Federal government enforce due process, civil rights.
Health care	Retain Medicaid essentially as it is for now. (Further recommendations forthcoming.)	Make Medicaid available to all the poor right away.	Set up national health insurance scheme to include all the poor and "near poor."	No expansion. Continue current levels.
New welfare programs	Set up system to replace AFDC which would include all families with children, one- and two-parent alike.	Require all states to offer AFDC-UP for intact families. Expand the enrollment and payment levels of SSI.	Require all states to offer AFDC-UP. Expand the SSI program by liberalizing its disability definition and expanding coverage.	No new nationally mandated programs.
Minimum benefits	System replacing AFDC will be based on local costs of nationally mandated minimum consumption, that is, a national minimum benefit, though reflecting varying price levels.	Mandate a minimum benefit for AFDC and food stamps equal to 65%, then 70%, eventually 100% of poverty level.	Mandate AFDC and food stamp minimum of 67% of poverty level, rising to 100% over time.	No minimum benefit.
Services to children and families	Wide expansion of services, counseling, training, nutrition, health benefits, childcare, etc.	Wide expansion of services, counseling, training, nutrition, health benefits, childcare, etc.	Wide expansion of services, counseling, training, nutrition, health benefits, childcare, etc.	At discretion of local administrators, within current funding levels.

(Table continues)

TABLE 5–1 (continued)

	APWA	Babbitt	Cuomo	White House
Teen-age pregnancy	More of the conventional services and interventions. Require completion of education.	Much more of the conventional services and interventions, plus provide more youth employment.	Much more of the conventional services and interventions.	Consider role of welfare in fostering teen pregnancy.
Child support enforcement	Determine paternity swiftly and enforce support payment on absent parents.	Determine paternity swiftly and enforce support payment on absent parents.	State guarantees minimum child support benefits. Uniform awards schedule. Automatic wage withholding.	No mention.
Education	Strengthen public schools.	Strengthen elementary and secondary schools. Reduce high school dropout. Expand vocational education.	Mainly, greatly expand Headstart-type programs. Begin at ages 3–4. Also, improve inner-city schools. Improve adult education. Use anti-drop-out incentives.	Must improve education to create future opportunities.
Work	Mandate workfare. Include heavy training and services. All with children 3 + obligated.	Require workfare to the extent "consistent with family responsibilities." Services provided.	Mandate workfare. Including training and services. Parents with young children allowed	Requiring work at state level seems successful.

78

	With younger children, part time. Federal government pays 75%.	"Provision" for a paid job. Private sector and regular public sector jobs preferred.	but not required. Guaranteed subsidized job if unable to hold private job.	
Paying for it	Phase new expenditures in gradually, over 10 years. There will be new costs for both federal government and states. View as an investment.	Tax income currently not subject to taxation. Cut nonwelfare programs to pay for substantial new costs.	Phase in gradually. As programs work, there may be savings. In the long run, competitiveness and justice require substantial new expenditures.	Hold spending constant at current level. Work for decrease in long run as programs work.
Making welfare programs transitional	Welfare should be disbursed in the context of "a 'discharge' plan aimed at eventual self-sufficiency and independence from the system."	Emphasis should shift from building welfare "safety net" to building "ladders" on which the poor can climb out of poverty and off government programs.	Open-ended, long-term welfare should end for the able-bodied, to be replaced by a time limited (perhaps 3 years maximum) transitional program, followed by a subsidized work-for-benefits program for those who have not gotten jobs by the end of the first stage.	"The true test of effectiveness of any governmental public assistance system should be measured by how many recipients become independent."

None calls for wholesale or comprehensive dismantling of existing programs, although all suggest letting many new experiments and new combinations of programs go forward.

Just the same, the White House Report does attack the centralizing *administrative* role played by the federal government, although not its funding role or its principle-setting role. By contrast, each of the other reports asks the federal government to set at least some new national standards—for example, a national minimum benefit level.

The White House Report rules out *any* new federal initiatives or new expenditures,[5] whereas each of the other three reports proposes at least some new federal expenditures and initiatives, sometimes of more than a modest or incremental sort. Here again, though, differences should not be exaggerated. In the current era of budget deficits, all four reports speak either of "revenue neutrality" (the White House) or of modest new expenditures (the other three reports), usually described as "investments" to be repaid by future savings. At those places where some of the reports call for expenditures that, in total, would be rather large, they at least have the integrity to call for tax increases or for compensating cuts in other, usually unnamed, parts of the federal budget.

There is a temptation to ascribe differences concerning the role of the federal government to ideology (or to principle, depending on whether one is describing the other's point of view or one's own). Consider these two rival and traditional images: a strong, active, caring federal government, on the one side, vs. an other-empowering, self-limiting, economy-liberating federal government, on the other. These are classic partisan differences. In the current debate on welfare, however, these two tendencies do not diverge extremely. Both sides speak of "partnership" between the federal government and the states and localities. Both sides recognize that the federal government has both the larger revenue base and the chief funding responsibility. Where, then, does the current disagreement lie?

The major point of dispute concerns where to establish certain standards and draw up regulations. The White House Report argues that it is counterproductive to do this from afar, centrally, when local communities diagnosing local needs with firsthand knowledge of their own people can make more realistic determinations. At least in certain matters if not all, the other reports would have the federal government establish national standards, national minimums, or national requirements.

Another difference is that some stress current ignorance, while others stress trying harder with existing programs. The White House Report tends to emphasize how much is *not* known about how to reduce dependency and, therefore, encourages many small experiments that might sort out what works from what does not work, before embroiling millions of citizens in national programs. The other reports tend to recommend enlargements of existing programs, with some modifications, in a spirit of rather greater confidence; yet, they too encourage experimentation and express their hopes with considerable caution. All have been chastened by the experience of the past twenty years, some more than others.

In an important sense, such disagreements are in large measure pragmatic. In principle, the White House Report recognizes the obligation of the federal government to impose clear national criteria: it states its own criteria at the beginning. In principle, the other reports recognize the need of states and localities for more discretion than at present, in order to take account of unique local circumstances. (The ethnic composition and urban concentrations of the poor in New York state, for example, are atypical of the nation as a whole, as the New York Report straightforwardly details.)

Still, each side has powerful reasons for arguing in particular cases whether there should be, or should not be, new national standards, national minimums, or national requirements. These reasons are usually practical. On such matters, persons of good will may often disagree.

This is not to deny that general ideological orientations and principled positions do play a role in such practical disagreements. Of course they do. At the same time, the White House Report says that the criterion by which its proposals should be judged, some five years or so hence, is whether they have actually helped to reduce dependency. An analogous criterion is also stated or suggested by each of the other reports.

Thus, our Working Seminar persists in its belief that current disagreements actually fall far more clearly in the domain of practicality than in the domain of principle or ideology. This observation may not reduce the fury of argument. But it should help to focus debate upon the one criterion of most benefit to the poor: which alternative is more likely to work?

There is another major difference. More resolutely than the other three reports, the White House Report is willing to continue welfare funding at current levels but not much higher. The other three reports are cautious in making new claims upon the federal budget in the light of current budget deficits, but they do make them, calling either for tax increases or for cuts in spending elsewhere. Two reasons are given for these requests for additional spending. First is the belief that more preschool education, more child care, more job training, and the like will produce results and are good investments. Second is the fallback belief that, even if such programs do not work out as predicted, such interventions must at least be tried.

The authors of the White House Report do not share the first belief, because of past experience. Regarding the second belief, they hold that new experiments should, indeed, be tried by the states and localities—and then, if successful, be imitated elsewhere. The argument, to repeat it, is that we do not yet know enough about what will actually work and should not venture vast experiments until some of the various models already being tested locally bear fruit. When that happens, the expansion of successful programs can then be paid for out of savings that accrue, as citizens cease being dependent, become productive, and pay taxes—and thus, in their turn, help to support others less fortunate than they. It is in the nature of experiments that some, even many, will fail; wisdom therefore suggests moving with surer, rather than with lesser, knowledge.

A broad consensus also seems to be forming among state welfare administrators concerning the elements of successful welfare reform. The new strategy is a blend of conservative and liberal themes. It includes a new emphasis on training and other services for poor persons, and it is also job-focused, taking as its premise the idea that all able-bodied persons ought to work. It is obligational, requiring aid recipients to meet certain responsibilities in return for their benefits. And it is "devolutional," relying heavily on state and local initiative.

Since 1981, the states have taken up this new challenge with vigor and in advance of congressional initiatives. Beginning with provisions in that year's budget act that authorized experiments in "community work experience programs," more than two-thirds of the states have initiated efforts along the lines sketched out above. Among them are California, Illinois, Massachusetts, West Virginia, Oklahoma, New Jersey, and Arkansas.

The California scheme appears to be the most highly developed. An agreement between the Republican governor and Democrats in the legislature led to a fundamental restructuring of the state's welfare system, shifting its orientation from a payment and social service system to one, in the words of Richard Nathan, "strongly oriented towards training, education, job placement and work—including in some cases the assignment of welfare family heads to obligatory work."[6]

These state efforts are very young. They must be considered experimental. Still, early research suggests that such programs may result in moderate but consistent increases in earnings for poor people and decreases in welfare payments. More significantly, proponents think, these initiatives show promise of "detoxifying" welfare both as an influence on personal habits and as a political issue.

This new resourcefulness in the states is not limited to the welfare arena; a broadly based school reform effort has also been spreading across the country. Since 1983 nearly every state has enacted at least some significant changes in its educational system under the influence of the movement for "educational excellence." States such as Tennessee, Florida, New Jersey, Missouri, Illinois, Mississippi, North Carolina, and California have notable programs. A wide range of tactics has been employed, including mechanisms to sort and grade teachers on merit and improve their pay, curriculum improvement, stiffer graduation requirements, remedial programs, recognition of high achievers and special classes for them, the establishment of specialized high schools, better mechanisms for educational financing, plans to integrate local businesses with school support, longer school days and years, and, in a few states, policies that allow poorly functioning school districts to be declared "bankrupt."

These policies are too new to be definitively appraised. Broad agreement, however, has been achieved concerning goals and general strategies. Taken together, these efforts—almost. entirely state initiated—constitute what P. Michael Timpane, president of the Teachers College at Columbia University, has called "a veritable revolution in elementary and secondary education policy."[7] Significantly, many of these plans have taken special pains to assist schools in those high-poverty areas where the children of the most vulnerable are often concentrated.

In summary, the members of the Working Seminar have been struck by the way in which the ideological dimensions of the current debate concerning family and welfare have been diminished. The pragmatic question, What will work? has rapidly gained ground.

There is now unanimity that dependency must be reduced. The one remaining question is how to do so. In turning to that decisive question, the Working Seminar is unanimous in recommending a pragmatic rather than an ideological approach. Within our seminar, although still in much disagreement, we have benefited greatly from listening to each other. We suspect that all citizens might also benefit by hearing out the arguments of those with whom they disagree.

Where Do We Go from Here?

In principle, programs are already in place for ending poverty completely among the elderly. To make certain that all the elderly are above the poverty line is already the express will of the people. Counting noncash benefits, by some measures the poverty rate for the elderly is down to 3 percent. Still, there are some who may be isolated, who may not know English, or who for other reasons may not be receiving benefits that the nation has intended for their relief.[8] Similarly, too, there is an express national will concerning the physically or mentally disabled. On these matters, there is little argument.

The low income of poor *nonelderly singles*, about 4 million strong, is also in principle soluble in a straightforward fashion. A full-time job at the minimum wage produces an income above the poverty line (approximately $5,500) for a single person. That some proportion of singles has missed out in developing the habits, attitudes, and aptitudes necessary to their own maintenance does not exclude them from compassionate attention; yet their own obligations to themselves and to the public cannot be passed over. Able persons have a responsibility to prepare themselves for, to find, and to keep jobs sufficient to their needs. About one-third of all such singles are between the ages of eighteen and thirty-four. Far from being supported by others, they should be coming to the support of those less able to care for themselves.

Most of the poor, we have seen, live in *families*. For *childless couples*, including those whose children are grown and gone, the poverty line is approximately $7,000 a year— not far above the income from one full-time job at the minimum wage. Two adults sound of mind and body ought to be able to support themselves at such a level. For *able parents with children*, about two-thirds of the poor, our survey of the existing statistics suggests five categories: (1) those who, although technically below the poverty line, live where and as they do voluntarily, are functioning well, and give evidence of high morale; (2) those married-couple families with children that two full-time jobs at the minimum wage would still not bring over the poverty line; (3) those female heads of families who through a change in marital status are temporarily thrown below the poverty line, but whose maturity, acquired skills, and habits have them poised for self-reliance, as soon as they overcome the sudden, temporary difficulties in which they find themselves; (4) those female heads of families who over long periods are intermittently but frequently dependent upon welfare; and (5) those very young female heads of families (teen-agers or barely more) who are at the beginning of potentially frequent spells on welfare.

Those in the first category are voluntarily poor and, as such, are not of immediate concern to public policy. Those in the second category, husband-wife couples who work full time and still fail to lift

84

their families above the poverty line, are nonetheless in a better position to lift their children and themselves out of poverty than families with one or no income earners. How to help working married-couple families is not, however, self-evident. The negative income tax, for example, had intuitive appeal to many analysts from several philosophical camps, until large-scale experiments with income supports revealed undesirable consequences, not least for family stability and increased welfare burdens. On the hopeful side, the elimination of federal income tax burdens embodied in the tax law of 1986 and the already scheduled raising of tax exemptions for dependents may, in combination, significantly improve the condition of two-earner couples, and an analogous lifting of state and local tax burdens would further help.

Concerning female heads of families who need temporary help in bridging the sudden income shortfall that sometimes accompanies a change in marital status, there is virtually universal consensus that temporary help under Aid to Families with Dependent Children is in order. To be sure, AFDC was first designed for widows; but nowadays divorce and separation are far more common reasons for financial distress among mothers, who more often than not in such cases retain custody of their children. Undoubtedly, the primary responsibility for income support to the children remains with the children's father, and much more needs to be done by way of changes in law and legal practice to hold fathers responsible for income support until the children are grown. When necessary, nonetheless, for mothers of the maturity, education, and skills described, there is a clear warrant for temporary public assistance.

Regarding female heads of families who have been dependent upon welfare intermittently for many years, two dangers have become apparent. First, long-term dependency tends to become a component of further personal decisions; second, habitual dependency tends to have harmful effects upon both the children of recipients and their own self-esteem. Most experts have a strong feeling that children ought not to be penalized by sanctions imposed upon their mothers (and, if their identity is known, as is almost always the case, upon their fathers). Most observers are also aware, however, that children are not helped by remaining in the care of mothers whose own habits are not responsible.

In such matters, public policy experts wish they had the wisdom of Solomon. Failing that, many recognize that the incentives built into current law and practice are not now reinforcing a sense of responsibility and obligation. Therefore, an emerging consensus holds that such benefits must be limited in duration and, second, that in exchange for benefits received such mothers ought to work, perhaps after receiving time-limited job training.

There is a further consensus that the isolation in which such women often live ought to be broken, preferably by private social or religious agencies that give instructions in child care, in self-help, and in preparation for employment. Further, some experts believe that some of the incentives in current programs, far from facilitating marriage or remarriage, make the latter more difficult. To reverse these trends, more needs to be done to bring about conditions in which marriage or remarriage becomes as highly probable among the poor as among the nonpoor, on the grounds that the two-earner household is far more likely to exit from poverty.

There is considerable debate about how old the children of welfare mothers ought to be before an obligation to earn income through work outside the home is legally imposed. This debate has been somewhat recast in recent years because so many nonpoor mothers with children under three years of age are now employed. Thus, the current consensus has moved rather decisively in the direction of lowering the age of youngest children at which welfare mothers would be required to work or to enroll in limited-duration training for employment.

Among other kinds of work for which such mothers can be trained (which would in turn assist them in bringing up their own children) are child care and preschool education. In most cities, where female heads of families tend to be concentrated, hotels and other service establishments have many needs for entry-level employees; and many also seek reliable long-term employees for positions of responsibility. Since there may be a tendency for experts to think of middle-class rather than of working-class jobs, even though the latter may pay as well and offer greater long-term possibilities, many training programs seem to be aimed at factory or office jobs, while overlooking the opportunities that immigrants find so helpful in gaining a foothold.

Concerning the fifth category above, female heads of families who are teen-agers or barely more, especially those who have borne children out of wedlock, public policy faces three distinct tasks. The first is to reduce the incidence of behaviors that lead to long-term dependency. The second is to intervene early enough with young mothers to help them exit from dependency quickly and later stay away from it. The third is to look to the well-being of their children, for whom some are ill equipped to give proper care.

Since in preceding generations there were lower proportions of children born out of wedlock, fewer teen-age pregnancies, and many fewer female-headed families, there is no cause to believe that current practices will always be with us. To grow to their current proportions required many changes in ethos and public practices. But social change has by no means come to an end, and since human beings are not helpless before inexorable forces of either "progress" or "decline," a determined generation can substantially affect the directions of social change. Teen-age pregnancy and out-of-wedlock birth are behaviors of serious consequence to society. A culture that says so, loud and clear, is likely to witness a reduction in their frequencies, and for the major institutions of society *not* to say so loud and clear would be irresponsible.

Furthermore, teen-age pregnancy and out-of-wedlock births, some evidence shows, are frequently not "accidental" but desired.[9] Often such behavior appears to spring from feelings of low esteem, a need for self-importance and love, and a form of bonding with a partner, however impermanent, that goes beyond merely sexual expression. To that extent, teen-age pregnancy and out-of-wedlock births are moral statements and need to be addressed in moral terms. At the very least, the Working Seminar believes that the relatively recent high frequency of such behaviors deserves dispassionate study, within appropriate moral as well as merely behavioral frameworks.

It also seems to be a less than adequate public policy, except in emergency cases, to allow teen-agers to establish separate households simply because of an out-of-wedlock birth. There are two reasons for this judgment. First, teen-agers are ill prepared to carry the weighty responsibilities of child care in isolation; second, "being married to welfare" should not be an available option for someone that young. A firm public message needs to be sent that public assistance in such cases can be only temporary and does not represent a long-term invitation to a dependent way of life. Setting up an independent household is the prerogative of those who have shown a capacity for maintaining their own independence.

There is a universal consensus that fathers bear responsibility for supporting their own children. From this it follows that both timely paternity findings and a body of legal practice effectively holding fathers responsible are very much in order.

Such reflections as these upon the data presented in part two illustrate the validity of the seven starting places made explicit in part one. First, we emphasized economic growth—the indispensable foundation for maintaining hope, for creating new jobs and opportunities, for providing necessary revenues, and for inspiring cooperation and mutual assistance throughout the republic.

Second, we saw that only through disaggregating the poor could one begin to devise programs designed to help them in the multiple ways appropriate to their variety.

Third, the programs begun in the 1960s and before have had remarkable success among the elderly; yet, with regard to behavioral dependency, they have not supplied effective remedies. The new emphasis today is necessarily upon behavioral dependency, not least —but not solely—upon the underclass.

What is distinctive about behavioral dependency is its moral or attitudinal component, manifest in an inability to cope on the part of many able-bodied adults. Two of its major causes are, on the one hand, female-headed households and, on the other, nonwork. In these two areas in particular, little progress can be made in reducing dependency apart from a heightened sense of personal responsibility.

Yet moral behavior seldom springs from resolute individual will alone. It usually requires the social support of major institutions reinforcing what is good and noble in human behavior and blaming what is not. A weak social ethos increases the probability of personal failures. A strong ethos nourishes and strengthens individuals who act responsibly and blames those who do not—and thereby affects the probable distributions of each. Relatively recent changes in behavior regarding crime, work, education, sexual behavior, marriage, and other facets of life are intertwined in the current profile of dependency. These changes in behavior do not spring from random individual choices alone; they appear to have been reinforced by massive changes in the nation's social ethos. To alter for the better the moral signals transmitted by our major institutions, both governmental and private, will also require massive efforts. For the moral signals its major institutions transmit, too, a free people is responsible.

In these matters, virtually every line of thought and every bit of evidence leads back to the family. Almost 80 percent of the poor live in families; 60 percent live in families with children under eighteen. To reduce dependency among able adults, especially those with children, is to help nurture models of self-reliance among those closest to the young, who are in turn the future carriers of our nation's destiny.

This nation depends in a critical way upon habits of self-reliance and cooperation. Should it cease to be a commonwealth of self-reliance, it would very soon cease to be "the home of the free." Thus, the new determination to reduce dependency offers an opportunity that must not be lost.

This is the context, and the spirit, in which we have formulated the following recommendations.

Notes

1. John F. Kennedy, "Special Message to the Congress on Public Welfare Programs," *Public Papers of the Presidents of the United States* (Washington, D.C.: Office of the *Federal Register*, National Archives and Record Service, 1953–), p. 103.

2. Editorial, *New York Times*, February 2, 1962.

3. See Blanche Bernstein, *Saving a Generation* (New York: Priority Press Publications, 1986), p. 13.

4. Two large philosophical points emerge in the Cuomo and the Babbitt reports. Both enunciate support for national health insurance—an issue that goes far beyond the immediate context of concern for poverty and dependency. And the Babbitt report, further, invokes a principle of relative equality by suggesting that the EITC should be indexed to a ratio of the median family income. Such a principle goes well beyond concern for a decent standard of living for the poor. To that concern it adds concern for relative equality in incomes. This will be resisted by those who favor help for the poor but are opposed to the egalitarian principle, holding that egalitarian schemes are necessarily artificial and coercive. Since the issues of national health insurance and egalitarian income schemes transcend the issues of poverty and dependency, we have preferred to emphasize the larger consensus upon the latter, rather than the obvious divisiveness of the former.

5. Subsequent to the White House Report, the President's Fiscal Year 1988 Budget proposal of January 1987 contained at least one new work and education program for welfare recipients. The new Greater Opportunities through Work ("GROW") program, to be administered by the states, would emphasize continuation in school, attainment of high school diplomas, employment-directed training, job search, and employment. Payments to the states for the program are estimated at $110 million in the budget.

6. Richard P. Nathan, "The Underclass: Will It Always Be with Us?" (Paper presented at the New School for Social Research, November 14, 1986), p. 20.

7. P. Michael Timpane, foreword to Denis P. Doyle and Terry W. Hartle, *Excellence in Education* (Washington, D.C.: American Enterprise Institute, 1985), p. xii.

8. See Spencer Rich, "Daily Needs Not Met for Many Elderly," *Washington Post*, January 17, 1987.

9. See Leon Dash, "Motherhood the Hard Way," *Washington Post*, January 27, 1986.

PART THREE
Dealing with Behavioral Dependency

6

A Community of Self-Reliance

Despair and Hope

At times, the problems of dependency seem overwhelming. When one thinks of all the cash shortfalls, educational needs, crime-wracked surroundings, disabilities, and health needs among the 33 million poor—and of the inadequate education, inability to cope, self-defeating behaviors, and dispiritedness that some of them experience—it sometimes seems that problems of dependency, going far beyond what can be solved with money, are impossibly immense.

In a different frame of mind, one recalls all the many citizens who have triumphed over circumstance; and one runs through one's mind the many resources American society already has in place for helping others to do the same. In such moments one may also have the vision of how things could be if the major institutions of American life were already doing their assigned jobs well. For example, education through elementary school and high school is free; attendance until age sixteen is mandatory. If such opportunities were being universally seized, so that every man, woman, and child in America were adequately educated in all the basic skills and ready to enter the world of work with the habits and aptitudes needed for employability, the road to long-term dependency would be far less traveled.

Almost 2 million new jobs are being created each year, and entry-level jobs are plentiful and open to all, as millions of immigrants are discovering. In some localities, labor markets are severely depressed, and thus economic growth is necessary. Still, where entry-level jobs are available, if all who were able to work took such jobs, even menial ones at first, stayed employed, and built up skills and proficiency, long-term dependency would be significantly reduced.

Marriage and family life are freely chosen. If a lasting husband-wife marriage were again the almost universal national choice and if young persons delayed having children until they had completed school, married, and established themselves in adequate employment, dependency would fall.

To develop sound habits and attitudes is the central art of living; acquiring them is crucial for success in every walk of life. If the nation's media—its rock stars, popular entertainers, and commentators on morals—sounded a drumbeat of hard work, responsibility, and a sound family life, the efforts of parents to teach their children the basics of self-reliance would be greatly strengthened. If religious institutions and schools taught self-respect and self-discipline and if local groups insisted on excellence and civility, then young persons, trying to meet the expectations of the adult world around them, would doubtless fulfill many more of their possibilities.

Having a low income is one thing when most of the poor have hope for a better life for themselves and their children and are trying to realize those hopes. It is quite another when millions, especially among the young, are passive in the face of opportunities available to them and fail to gain the skills to act productively, even on their own behalf and when many nongovernmental institutions of American life are failing to provide the local, concrete leadership needed to break these self-damaging behaviors.

For such reasons, the Working Seminar emphasizes strongly that, in the next round of assaults upon the problems of poverty, government assistance alone is not enough. *All the institutions of American society will need to become engaged in supporting the struggle of the poor for self-reliance and participation in the common life.* At every level—from those who help to shape the national ethos, to clergy, parents, and teachers in local schools who teach our young high morale, character, and determination—Americans must recreate our two-sided ideal of community and self-reliance. Our bonds to each other must be strengthened. The capacity of each to develop the skills required for independence must be exercised.

What can our institutions do to bring this about? Some of the poor are elderly, disabled, or otherwise objectively in need of income support. Providing income support to such needy persons is not without its unintended consequences; still, compared with treating the problems of those whose dependency is behavioral, it is relatively straightforward. Others—the able poor of working age and their children—need skills, habits, and attitudes through which to achieve independence and make the productive contributions society needs from them. Still others have deeper problems, such as drug abuse. No complex society will ever want for persons who need a full range of special attention, well beyond an income supplement. Their unusually large numbers today, however, have led the Working Seminar to concentrate far more upon the behaviorally dependent than upon the

94

traditional vulnerable ones such as the elderly and the disabled.

The nation need not be concerned if low income results from a voluntary choice, but only if dependency is not voluntary. Income support, when families and private sources cannot provide it, is mainly government's responsibility; dependency and dysfunction require much more than that—and from the whole society. This added attention cannot be given impersonally. Most of it must be given by concerned individuals: parents, teachers, clergymen, fellow parishioners, employers, journalists, medical assistants, and other citizens. Dependency has many human dimensions; that is what makes it seem intractable. We applaud the work of community groups, sensitive to local needs and able to draw upon resources not available to any government, in giving encouragement and concrete assistance to persons seeking to better their own condition. We encourage their expansion.

But government, too, must look to its own expenditures on behalf of the income support and the educational, health, and human services it offers to its citizens. The federal government alone is spending more than $400 billion annually for such purposes, although mostly (and most successfully) for retirees. State and local governments spend many further billions. Government must be certain that the present design of its programs is actually achieving its own good intentions. This will require a transformation of the nation's flawed entitlement-based system into a system that emphasizes the mutuality of assistance and obligation.

Like other institutions, government is a limited and less than perfect instrument. Like medicine, for those it means to help it should not make things worse. And it should frequently look afresh at its own work. Its new initiatives should be measured by careful reflection on past results. As experience warrants, changes of direction will be called for.

Our recommendations, then, are aimed at every institution of American life. Some are designed to enable government—federal, state, and local—to do better what only government can do. These are discussed in the following chapters.

The Foundation:
A Growing Economy

In principle, no one will disagree that the foundation of successful welfare reform is *economic growth*. Economic growth is indispensable to an atmosphere of hope, to economic opportunity, to the creation of jobs, and to growing public revenues. As Alice M. Rivlin has written:

The experience of the postwar period indicates that overall economic growth is a powerful means of reducing poverty. Programs to provide education and job skills for low-income people have little chance of success if there are few jobs available and little prospect of a better income. Even if some proportion of those in poverty cannot be expected to participate in income growth, the provision of resources for their support is easier with a growing economy. [1]

As we learned the hard way during the mid-1970s and during the recessions of 1980 and 1981–1982, when the economy goes badly, little else goes well, especially for the poor and the dependent. By contrast, those periods during which poverty has most declined have invariably been periods of economic growth. Clearly, policies designed to reduce poverty must be consistent with economic growth.

Some commentators have expressed concern about apparent inequalities in the distribution of income and wealth in our society. We share their desire for fair distribution but remain convinced that only economic growth meets broad human needs for progress, including better distribution. It is in times of economic growth that the poor increase their shares.

Despite the recent long-lived economic recovery, some experts have contended that an expanding economy is not helping the large numbers of the poor who live in distressed areas where jobs are not likely to be plentiful. This, too, is not beyond dispute. Areas of concentrated poverty are clearly in evidence, but just how hopeless their problems really are is not a settled question. In recent years, the American economy has generated millions of new jobs, including many in communities (such as the old mill towns of New England and the small cities of the South) for which hope had been all but abandoned just a few years earlier.

Moreover, the high rates of employment found among recent immigrants suggest that entry-level positions even in high-poverty areas are not lacking; and the fact that only a minority of the poor reports that work is unavailable tends to confirm the point. In any event, the fact that some areas need more concentrated attention is no reason to resist policies that favor a broad and general pattern of economic growth. The latter will in any case be necessary, even if only to gain resources for tackling the harder cases.

Nonetheless, a significant proportion of the poor is not benefiting sufficiently from recent economic growth. The number of single-parent families without income earners (or only low earners) has grown quite large during the past fifteen years; and young singles are remaining outside the labor force in proportions seldom seen before.

96

Economic growth occurs around them, and, while many benefit, others seem unable to take advantage of new opportunity. By not working, such citizens are denying themselves a crucial form of personal development, a sense of responsibility, and the satisfactions of self-mastery; and the community is denied the positive contributions they could make. To change this novel situation, however, economic growth remains indispensable, even though it is not sufficient.

Our Working Seminar does not recommend specific economic policies, only some fundamentals. Inflation hurts the poor and those on fixed incomes most of all; keeping it low is basic. Job growth is crucial if the poor are to contribute to society and share in its wealth with fairness and dignity. Enterprise and investment are necessary if the poor are to improve their lot.

The only solid foundation on which the poor can be helped is economic growth. Yet, since economic growth is not sufficient to meet the problems of dependency and dysfunction, which are at the roots of the present crisis, we have been driven back to some other fundamentals too.

Note

1. Alice Rivlin, ed., *Economic Choices 1984* (Washington, D.C.: Brookings Institution, 1984), p. 3.

7

Recommendations

Dealing with Behavioral Dependency

If the problem faced by the nation were solely that of raising the incomes of the poor to levels above the poverty line, its task would be merely monetary. Nor is it especially difficult to help those able adults who for reasons beyond their control, for limited periods of time, need help to regain their own self-reliance. Resources exist for such matters; procedures have been tested in the crucible of hard experience. There are always shortages of time, personnel, and money in existing social service agencies, but for those adults at the margin of the working community the prognosis is good.

The most baffling problem is how to help those adults who in principle *should* be earning their own way out of poverty but who now lack the capacity to help themselves. They may be of sufficient age, health, and objective capacity; yet, nonetheless, they are not coping. Possibly, their own basic institutions—families, schools, churches, neighborhoods, the economy, or even the ethos informing their knowledge of life—have failed them. Or, possibly, they have failed to live up to the standards of the institutions that have tried to help them. Some of the poor, as we have seen, report that it is too easy to interpret current welfare programs as an offer of cash and assistance, medical and nutritional, on condition that one chooses to have children and not to marry.

A free society levies demands on individuals; it offers opportunities, but no one is coerced into taking advantage of them; it permits failure. For whatever mixture of reasons, circumstantial or personal, there seem today to be significant numbers of citizens whose own behavior is putting them, and keeping them, in dependency upon the public purse—and, worse still, in an inward dependency, which prevents them from coping well with responsibilities even to themselves. Alcoholism and drug abuse are obvious manifestations; others are dropping out of school, regarding work (beyond hustling or street crime) as foreign territory, or failing to pursue long-term goals of self-development. Some young people are begetting children out of wedlock and before they are ready for the responsibilities of parenthood, thus involving many innocents in cycles of vulnerability. For such persons, low income is in a sense the least of their problems; a failure to take responsibility for themselves and for their actions is at the core. It would seem to be futile to treat the symptom, low income, rather than the fundamental need, a sense of self.

The matter is so basic that it is hard to know where to begin, except with basics. In a free society, a broadly diffused *sense of personal responsibility* is an essential component of a vital public life. Without it, the institutions of a free society could no longer function, and individuals would fail to live as free men and women.

But how do most citizens learn the sense of self that comes from assuming responsibilities, setting goals, accomplishing first one task and then another, and thus enjoying the pleasures of self-determination? And what can other citizens do to help those who face difficulty in taking such steps? Mostly, we do not think about these things because the institutions that surround us teach them to us so effectively that we hardly notice. It is only when this basic teaching breaks down that we recognize what we once took for granted—like learning to walk again after an accident. It is this breakdown that helps to explain the approach that we have taken.

First, for child development, for sound habits, for assistance in schoolwork, for income, for mutual support in work—in a multitude of ways—the *family* occupies a pivotal point in social life. During a child's formative years, family life profoundly influences whether the practice of personal responsibility is reinforced or undermined. Thus, much of the success of public policy depends upon what it can assume families will do, or not do. The better the family functions, the easier it is for other institutions. When families exhibit deficiencies, the work of other institutions, trying to make up the deficits, is more difficult and more complex.

Second, in complex societies such as ours, *education* in school and continuing in later life is critical for personal development, for growth in the habits of citizenship, and for self-mastery.

Third, for able adults, *work* is the basic route to self-reliance and a sense of dignity; it is also one of the chief ways by which individuals contribute to the common good of all.

Fourth, *voluntary social institutions* play crucial public roles: in shaping the effective social ethos within which citizens learn to exercise their responsibilities, in establishing the environment within which government operates, and in conducting the main activities of

99

civilized peoples: commerce, science, the arts, civic discourse, play, and worship. The scope of voluntary social institutions is larger, and more basic, than the scope of government—clearly so in the realm of conscience, ideas, and information; in the world of work; and even in the actual carrying out of public policy. The multiple roles of the press, the arts, religious institutions, educators, businesses, unions, and every sort of association and organization have a larger public sweep than the roles properly assigned to government.

Nonetheless, *the federal government, state governments, and local governments* have been assigned fundamental tasks that, although strictly limited, are indispensable to the common good. These various levels and forms of government best work in partnership, without usurping one another's proper spheres. Obviously a degree of potential conflict has deliberately been built into the system, for the sake of creativity and for checking abuse, sloth, and other faults to which institutions are prey. Sometimes one among them, sometimes another, may represent the cutting edge of the nation's moral sense.

All these basics—personal responsibility, family, education, work, voluntary social institutions, and every level of government—have been important in our thinking about the behavioral dependencies that keep too many able adult citizens from acting well upon their own behalf—keep them dependent upon the public purse, in the first place, and keep them unable to cope well for themselves. The problems of dependency and dysfunction are so basic that they can scarcely be addressed otherwise. Government alone cannot solve these problems; it can scarcely even touch them at their depths. But government can show leadership in focusing upon them candidly and realistically, in inspiring all citizens and all institutions of society to focus their talents and resources upon desperate needs, and in helping to set in place the conditions that may lead to steady and sound progress in reducing them. As far as the Working Seminar can see, there is no silver bullet, no magic wand. The existing problems are deep, difficult, perhaps to some extent intractable. That they exist in current magnitudes, however, corrodes a free society.

In making our recommendations, accordingly, we have tried to stick close to basics and to hit the middle level of generality—to state clear principles, but without becoming bogged down in technical detail. There is still too much to learn through experimentation, demonstration, and research to make definitive programmatic suggestions with certainty. We have kept practicality in mind, but have seldom addressed the particulars of administration.

We have chosen this approach because the members of our

Working Seminar, representing several different philosophical orientations, have come to recognize that persons of good will, while disagreeing upon some particulars, may simultaneously stand together on essential common principles. The problems of dependency and dysfunction are today so at odds with what this country stands for, and so damaging to the citizens caught up in them, that a common assault upon them is absolutely indispensable. That is why we have tried to go beyond our diverse views in order to establish common ground.

The Working Seminar did not attempt to reach complete agreement among its members on the steps to be taken. Some in our group believe that the current welfare system has failed the test of any successful system: to provide needed assistance to those unable to help themseves, but without destroying the spirit, initiative, and drive of many others. The trends of the past decades represent in their view not failures that can be fixed by better program engineering, but the futility of attacking dependency at a distance. Nonetheless, short of a total restructuring of the welfare system, which now seems to them unlikely, they embrace the principles set forth by the Working Seminar.

Together, the entire Working Seminar holds that reducing dependency will require the keenest intelligence and most sustained effort American society can summon. It will require working together as a national community to increase the numbers of self-reliant citizens.

Major Agents of Change:
Family, Schools, Neighborhoods

1. *The home environment for young children in impoverished families should be the primary location for preventing future dependency.* During the crucial early years, the family is the most favorable place in which to show the young how to become conscientious, cooperative, and self-reliant citizens. When families lack that capacity, other institutions must come to their assistance. Some poor families have abundant capacity to give their children a nurturing environment and, by the same token, some wealthier families lack it. The challenges all parents face, however, are generally more burdensome for those who have inadequate incomes. That is why the large number of children in poverty—especially those in single-parent families—gives rise to deep concern. Some impoverished families, such as those concentrated in the high-poverty urban areas and sometimes referred to as the "underclass," endure especially severe deficits.

101

With all these needs in view, we offer the following recommendations:

- Religious institutions, schools, and voluntary institutions should make the moral, cultural, and educational enrichment of home life a primary focus of efforts to reduce dependency. Classes in child care, handbooks designed for parents who seek help in doing better, and outreach services should be developed.
- Parental responsibility for the support of children should be reinforced. Although the nation pays considerable homage to the notion that parents are responsible for the support and upbringing of their children, our practice in recent decades has fallen increasingly short of that ideal. Public policies have failed to support the exercise of this responsibility.
- Political and administrative pressure should be brought to bear to improve that record. Some would advocate allowing lawyers to accept child-support cases on a contingent-fee basis. Others argue that changes in the property aspects of divorce laws will be needed to undo provisions adopted in the past decade.
- The fathers of out-of-wedlock children receiving AFDC should be identified by mandatory paternity findings; all fathers should be held to child-support obligations, and efforts should be made to collect from them; and community leaders ought to hold up for esteem only those fathers who fulfill their family responsibilities.
- Young mothers receiving AFDC benefits should be required to complete their high school degrees or equivalency and then seek work.
- Voluntary institutions should help these young mothers through classes in child care and child education, and other efforts that bring these mothers out of isolation, in social settings that provide child care and instruction and also prepare them for employment. Such initiatives are under way in several states.
- In regard to young teen-age mothers, welfare policy should not confuse their legal status as parents with their physical and emotional standing, which may be less than adult. It is self-deception to suppose that allowing teen-agers to establish their own homes enables them to exercise parental responsibility. Consequently, unless there is a finding that their safety so requires, welfare benefits should not be paid to recipients under age eighteen living in independent households. Rather, recipients should be aided either in the homes of their own parents or in supervised congregate homes, such as those now being run by voluntary civil, religious, or other social service groups.
- Child abuse and child neglect are serious national problems.

102

There is a tendency, however, to treat the symptoms of poverty as a form of "child neglect." A large number of poor children now being placed in foster care could be safely left with their parents.

• Support should be given to organized private efforts such as one recently announced by a national coalition of black churches to encourage their members to open their homes for the adoption of parentless black children who would otherwise be sent to state foster care.

• Parent-teacher associations should develop materials and counseling services especially designed for parents in high-poverty areas to help them to strengthen the educational environment of the home, to design home study areas, and to prescribe hours for homework.

• Experiments in various localities to link schools to homes, especially among the dependent poor, should be studied for ideas that work, as should those experiments in early childhood education for the poor that have proved particularly effective.

• Instruction in the probable long-term effects of illegitimacy and early parenthood upon both children and their unprepared parents should be made available to families and schools, lest irresponsible pregnancies contribute to long-term dependency.

None of the members of the Working Seminar believes that the trends in divorce and illegitimacy that have so altered the American family in the past generation are inexorable, even though altering their direction may be difficult and slow. While those trends are no doubt more affected by cultural than by governmental factors, government should not reinforce developments fraught with social misery.

2. *Schools should impose high standards of achievement, behavior, and responsibility on all students.* Education is vital for all children, but especially so for those from disadvantaged backgrounds. Few public policy developments in the past twenty years have been as ruinous for the poor as the well-documented decline in the quality of American public schools. In the past, schooling was a powerful engine of upward mobility, enabling the young to overcome the disadvantages of impoverished backgrounds and to rise to heights their parents had barely imagined. Still today, there is a strong association between the completion of high school and the avoidance of lengthy periods in poverty. A large proportion of students, however, do not finish high school at all, and for students from low-income homes drop-out rates are particularly high.

Ironically, the decline in educational quality comes just at the time in which educational research has begun to identify the key

103

ingredients in successful schools. These ingredients were recently summarized, for example, by Secretary of Education William J. Bennett:

> [Successful] schools have outstanding principals who lead and inspire and bring out the best from a dedicated, motivated teaching staff. These schools reach out to parents and establish an alliance among the parents, the community, and the school: an alliance dedicated to the nurture, protection, and education of children.
>
> These schools concentrate on the basics—the basics of good behavior and the basics of academic achievement. They set rigorous standards for students. They nurture character and transmit clear standards of right and wrong. These schools reward all forms of achievement by students, and they provide regular assessments of students' progress so the children get the help and the support they need.[1]

Federal, state, and local funds alone cannot buy effective schools, because the participation of parents in the education of their children is indispensable. Nonetheless, along with other institutions of American society, government at all levels should concentrate on improving the effectiveness of local schools. On the one hand, behavioral dependency among parents is associated with poor performance by their children in schools. On the other hand, a sound basic education secures for children the surest escape from cycles of dependency.

• Communities should be encouraged and assisted in setting high standards for their schools, recognizing that the key factors are strong principals, an orderly but not rigid school atmosphere, a schoolwide commitment of resources to and focus on basic skills, a highly visible expectation that every child can learn, and frequent monitoring of the performance of each student.

• Great care should be taken in choosing principals, and rewards should go to those who are particularly successful in setting high standards and in leading students to achieve them.

• The training of principals should be a high community priority.

• Fear of lawsuits claiming the violation of "student rights" has deprived some school officials of a spirit of initiative and has led others to take the course of least resistance, for example, by not enforcing standards of behavior that they know have been violated. Federal law should be amended so that, within appropriate limits, principals have greater good-faith discretion in setting and enforcing schoolwide standards of behavior, without fear of law suits.

- Since there is abundant evidence that family life has a profound —even decisive—impact on what a child learns, educators must make a more serious and sustained effort to involve parents in the education of their children. To be successful with disadvantaged children, in particular, schools must involve families in the day-to-day business of education: doing homework, specifying expectations, maintaining intellectual and physical discipline, and monitoring performance. In addition, parents must ensure that the climate at home complements and reinforces that at school and that both together reward solid achievement and excellence.

- An important step in this direction, consistent with racial integration and systemwide order, would be to give parents a greater measure of choice regarding which public schools their children attend, as is now done with "magnet" or specialized schools.

- The choice of an appropriate educational program for their children is especially important for low-income families. Some members of the Working Seminar favor a voucher or an open enrollment plan; others doubt the practicality of such plans. All agree in seeking ways to give poor parents more of the flexibility and freedom others already have and to make the public schools more accountable for their performance among the poor.

- Although most of the burden for improving education lies with state governments and local communities, the federal government has expressed its own concern through various programs. There is some evidence to suggest that these efforts have had at least some good effects, not as deep and lasting as had been hoped, but warranting experiments and demonstrations designed to do better than the early ventures.

- Since teen-age pregnancy is a significant cause of dropping out of high school (as well as of a future of welfare dependency), much recent discussion has been devoted to what schools might be able to do to prevent it. For behavioral dependency, illegitimacy is a crucial issue. Some suggest earlier and more thorough sex education classes; others favor providing advice on contraceptives through school health services; some advocate moral education and character formation; still others believe that only strict methods such as expulsion from regular classes can have the needed impact on the values of all.

Some evidence suggests that pregnancy rates are most likely to decline when teen-agers have a strong sense of self-esteem and are optimistic about the future. If so, one of the most effective steps schools can take is to give teen-agers confidence in their own education and in their preparation for careers. Clearly, sexuality affects human beings in their complexity and raises moral, psychological, and emotional questions. In any case, the approach to these questions should serve the values important in reducing behavioral dependency: the married-couple family, personal responsibility, preparation for parenthood, and a respect for social obligations.

Education, of course, cannot carry the entire burden of reducing teen-age pregnancy or, for that matter, of alleviating dependency. The job of providing adequate instruction is difficult enough without making schools responsible for curing all the problems that afflict the unfortunate. But for schools to demand less of the children of the poor would be tragically wrong. Only by insisting on a high standard for all students can schools convey society's expectation that the poor are as competent as others and, given the strength of some in the face of adversity, sometimes more so.

3. *The rights of the poor to integrity of life, limb, and property should receive equal protection under law.* Crime and civic disorder are among the worries of most Americans, but they are part of daily life of the poor. The neighborhoods in which the poor live—especially the inner-city enclaves, not least in large public housing projects—are often wracked by violence and vandalism. Signs of decay and destruction, human as well as physical, are everywhere in sight.

Such conditions have a profound effect on residents who are seeking to escape from poverty, and not just because their lives and property are always in danger. In troubled neighborhoods, small stores and businesses—an important source of entry-level jobs—cannot flourish, and discipline in the schools breaks down. Those who do manage to get ahead move out as soon as possible, depriving those who remain of community leaders and role models. Despair and resignation are in the air, not the faith and optimism needed to sustain the quest for advancement.

One of the most fundamental goals of government is to preserve "domestic tranquillity." In the neighborhoods inhabited by the poor, public policy is falling far short of that basic objective. New directions are necessary:

• Innovative methods of policing, aimed at maintaining order, not just solving crimes, should be introduced.

• Court procedures, particularly with regard to bail, sentencing, and parole, should be tightened.

• The illegal drug trade in poverty-stricken communities should be controlled. In this task, broad community support at every level is necessary, including national leadership and massive support from the media of popular entertainment.

• Government can act directly and effectively to better neighborhood conditions by amending the rules regarding public housing. At present, these regulations make it extremely difficult to exclude or to evict tenants who do not meet minimally acceptable standards of conduct. This situation should be remedied.

• In some places, groups of public housing residents have been able to organize and enforce standards that have dramatically improved living conditions and safety. Public policy should encourage neighborhood crime patrols, sanitary code enforcement drives, school associations, and the like. Most communities, when challenged, do possess the leadership to sustain such activities; but beyond attaining immediate goals, successful local self-organization reinforces habits of social imagination and perseverance.

We are aware that recommendations of these types raise justifiable concerns about their potential for violating individual rights or unduly infringing upon unconventional behavior. As in other areas of public policy, a wise balance must be struck. Since in recent years public policy may have gone too far toward protecting personal rights of those who ignore community responsibilities, more concern must be given to the well-being of the large numbers of poor and dependent, whose chances for achieving a decent standard of living are undermined by the flagrantly disruptive conduct of irresponsible neighbors.

The Vital Sector:
Voluntary Institutions

Although in the past two decades all levels of government have assumed increased responsibilities for helping the poor and dependent, nonetheless the success of public efforts depends crucially upon what major private institutions do, including the media, religious institutions, professional organizations, voluntary associations, and others. Government can help create an economic and social climate that is conducive to self-reliance, but only private institutions can inculcate the values and habits, and establish the local supports, that enable people to achieve it. Laws and administrative regulations can enforce civic obligations and standards of good conduct, but only the support and encouragement of private institutions can make them a matter of internalized volition. A free people is responsible to moral principles far beyond the reach of government.

From the other direction, too, public policy can and does affect the character of private institutions. Welfare agencies inevitably con-

107

vey values, not solely material assistance. Schools inevitably convey values, not solely academic skills. In the settings of the poor and the dependent, many values currently conveyed are not as helpful as they ought to be. And many national institutions that have great influence upon the behavior of the poor may be chiefly attuned to the very different life styles of those who are better off.

Nonetheless, one of the worst handicaps of poverty-stricken communities is a breakdown in their own capacity to form associations of mutual support. As a result, many of today's poor live in a cultural climate that is deprived, and this deprivation goes deeper than economic insufficiency alone. All assistance to them should be designed in ways that evoke their own strengths, and never by assuming that these strengths do not exist.

The Working Seminar believes that, if the nation's revived interest in reducing poverty and dependency is not to fail, raising the confidence of the poor in their own innate strengths, values, and habits is of the highest priority. When society expects too little of each citizen, it encourages a habit of dependency.

In this respect, voluntary institutions must play the crucial role. A century and a half ago, Tocqueville recognized that association is the true invention of America and the first principle of the new science of democracy. "Public" and "private" are not antonyms; they are two distinct but related ways of expressing the social nature of human beings. Of the two, the nongovernmental public sphere is by its nature the larger, more central, more flexible, more immediate, and more inventive. Its responsibilities are more various and encompassing than those of government. Thus, questions of poverty and dependency cannot be confined solely to action by government, for the governmental sector is by its nature unable to engage such problems at the necessary moral depth. There follows a major principle.

4. *Since voluntary associations have a public character and public responsibilities, they should focus their power on reducing behavioral dependency.*

• The mass media, for example, have vast (but not unlimited) power to shape the national ethos and to focus public awareness on important problems, as they have done successfully with regard to world famine, fitness, smoking, and other issues. In the values they transmit, in the heroes they hold up for public acclaim, in the lessons they convey through songs and stories, and in other ways, the media can help nourish a moral environment in which the habits crucial to exiting from poverty are socially reinforced. The media must lead the way to a new national commitment to reducing dependency if that commitment is to succeed. Some of the young are more likely to derive their cultural heroes from the media than from their parents, teachers, religious traditions, or other local authorities.

• Since many of the poor, as well as the nonpoor, are devoutly religious, religious institutions are among the most effective institutions in impoverished communities, and have the potential to provide considerable personal guidance and practical help. When true to their own inherent power, few institutions can better inculcate those habits of cooperation and self-reliance, of responsibility, self-control, and community service that best express human dignity. Few can better address the current breakdown of religious ideals of marriage, fidelity, and commitment, which is not only wreaking unprecedented devastation among the poor, but also steadily increasing their numbers (even during periods of economic growth).

• Religious social agencies should help to focus the resources of society upon the moral dimensions of dependency. But at the same time, working from principles different from those of government officials, they should challenge the poor and empower them through spiritual determination, inner strength, and community involvement.

• Religious institutions should inspire the nonpoor to reach out to the poor in private and local ways. Whereas making up for income shortfalls is necessarily a task in which government must play by far the larger role, religious and other voluntary institutions can focus both philanthropy and charity on the family life of the vulnerable, the personal development of youth, and social cooperation in neighborhoods.

• Voluntary and professional associations—fraternal organizations, foundations, service clubs, citizens' committees, neighborhood organizations, businesses in their civic and philanthropic roles, and other social bodies—should strive to make up for the inevitable limitations of public policy.

• Using the talent and resources that are their glory, voluntary associations should continue to take inventory of the problems of the poor and the dependent in their communities and seek to invent new ways of coming to their aid. This should include diagnosing where government programs fall short, examining local civic resources, and restructuring local methods of meeting human needs, so that efforts now wasted (or not being undertaken at all) might be redirected in a more systematic and productive way.

• Beyond providing those charitable donations of goods and services that will always be necessary in any society, associations with particular skills should make contributions, flowing from their own strengths, that no one else is likely to meet.

• Lawyers and medical professionals have special obligations to the homeless, many of whom are clearly incapable of self-reliance and in need of medical treatment. Using private initiatives, bankers, builders, and realtors should address the housing needs of low-income families and encourage the private upgrading and improvement of the existing housing of the poor. One example of such projects is to sponsor neighborhood teams of craftsmen—who might not otherwise find credit—to purchase, rehabilitate, and resell or rent older buildings. As some are already doing, food distributors in metropolitan centers should devise private sector ways to make otherwise wasted food available to food banks for the hungry.

• Last, but not least, is the important role of specific organizations of ethnic and racial minorities. Although blacks and Hispanics are still disproportionately represented among the dependent, it is less plausible today than it was a generation ago to assert that poverty is especially connected with race. Today, nonetheless, the scholars, leaders, and rank-and-file members of black and other minority-group organizations are speaking frankly about behavioral dependency and devising realistic ways of dealing with it. Their leadership is indispensable to the social progress of all groups. They establish the tone and context of much public discussion. The nation relies heavily upon them.

• For all voluntary institutions, from religious institutions through philanthropic organizations to businesses, it is more than ever necessary to reach into the areas in which dependency is concentrated. Apart from habits of self-reliance, citizens in those areas cannot better their condition; yet interventions from government are likely to deepen them in dependency unless other citizens reach into their lives and draw them into the ethos of cooperation and self-reliance. It would be wrong now, more than ever, to abandon the underclass. Since federal programs are not sufficient to end dependency (and, when done badly, may permit it to thrive), it is crucial that other agencies become involved.

In summary, voluntary institutions play a broader and deeper role than government. But they alone, apart from government, cannot do all that is needed if dependency and dysfunction are to be reduced.

Federal, State, and Local Government

Not all Americans can support themselves, nor should they be expected to. Generous provision for those without other means is the clearly expressed will of our society. Yet unease has grown in recent years about the consequences of welfare programs. Across the political spectrum, concerns that we have not been doing enough have been eclipsed by fear that we may be doing the wrong things—and thus worsening (or at least, ineffectively responding to) the condition of the poor. As a result there has been a resurgence of interest in redesigning public assistance programs, with the aim of providing more adequate aid to the poor without inducing the values and habits characteristic of prolonged dependency.

In framing our own recommendations for governmental actions, we discovered on the one hand, to an extent that surprised us, that much of what used to be the conventional wisdom about a sound public assistance program is no longer broadly accepted. On the other hand, the shifting weight of evidence has made much that used to be controversial appear to be well founded. Focusing on basic principles reveals most starkly the outlines of the new consensus.

5. *Recipients of welfare should be required to take part in work (or time-limited training programs) as a condition of obtaining benefits.* For those who are able to become self-reliant, welfare policy should be designed to help them do so. Though somewhat controversial a decade ago, this principle is now widely accepted; states and localities throughout the country are experimenting with ways of implementing it through work and training programs. Many issues remain to be addressed.

First, who should be considered "able to become self-reliant"? Some would exempt mothers of preschool children and thereby eliminate a significant portion of the welfare population. Others would leave such decisions to the discretion of local officials and thereby ensure wide variations in enrollment. From our reading of the evidence, members of the Working Seminar generally believe that work programs should be broadly inclusive and have uniform standards of eligibility. Not even mothers of preschool children should be exempt, since a majority of their counterparts who do not receive welfare are in the labor force at least part time. Further, those who delay entry into the labor force will find it more difficult later.

A second issue concerns the kinds of work or training that should be undertaken by those who are expected to participate. Among existing work programs, the range of activities is broad, extending from elaborate social and educational services to rudimentary "work experience" assignments. We believe that such diversity is desirable, since to be successful a program must be attuned to the differences found among the poor and dependent. Further, such diversity adds to

111

our remarkably incomplete information about what does in fact work. The Manpower Demonstration Research Corporation and others have developed effective research methods for evaluating such experiments.

Whatever the case, it is essential that all able recipients should be enrolled in work, duration-limited education, or short-term training programs in return for collecting welfare benefits.

• Young mothers should be required to complete high school (or its equivalent) and prepare themselves for future employment.

• Older mothers with previous experience in the labor force should be expected to find work in the private sector or (as a last resort) to accept an assignment in the public sector.

• Those involved in work programs, whether staff or participants, should be expected to regard every job, even part time and at a minimum wage, as an obligation to society, as important to future work experience, and as an occasion of self-development. Without this conviction current efforts to provide new services to welfare recipients could, like many previous ones, become a substitute for work.

• A minimum of emphasis should be placed on public service jobs; the overriding emphasis should fall on personal responsibility for finding jobs in the private sector. Social service agencies, with strong political leadership, should develop programs to involve private sector employers in placement efforts. Jobs in government should be accepted reluctantly and only in areas so depressed that there are clearly insufficient jobs of any kind. In the growing service economy in the 1990s, entry-level jobs are likely to become increasingly abundant as labor shortages develop because of demographic factors. The coming decade may be unusually favorable for moving large numbers of recipients from welfare to work.

6. *The implementation of work programs should move forward cautiously and in graduated steps.* Over the past twenty years the experience of federal job training programs has been less than impressive. Although the current wave of innovative workfare experiments is of considerable social value, even these promise modest results. The danger is that excessive eagerness to move ahead with an idea that *seems* to work may put in place an expensive program that does not lessen dependency. Therefore, the Working Seminar recommends a step-by-step approach to workfare, securing sound successes and avoiding overpromising and disillusionment. Programs should be neither massive nor designed for swift results but designed for steady

progress in increasing the proportions of the employable engaged in constructive work. Various states and localities have already become laboratories of this approach.[2]

The funding formula between states and the federal government should maintain the incentive of states and localities to reap the benefits of the savings gained by moving the dependent from passive recipiency to productive work. The formula should place a high premium on strong and imaginative local leadership able to match individual job seekers with individual employers; in work programs this is crucial. If too large a portion of funding flows from the federal government, the incentives for state and local governments shift. Instead of husbanding their own hard-earned resources wisely and actually helping the dependent to gain independence, administrators may spend less carefully money on which they are themselves dependent. Considerations of fiscal responsibility and self-reliance bind various levels of government, too.

In candor it must be said that many people—including members of the Working Seminar—believe that the numbers of persons moving from dependency to work are likely to be modest at first, and some of those who do begin to work may have families too large to support without additional assistance. Nonetheless, even modest gains are not to be dismissed lightly; the benefits to each individual and family make important differences to their morale and sense of dignity. But more crucial still is the broader *signaling* aspect of public policy. Public policy establishes a moral climate as well as an economic one; it sets goals for citizens and incites efforts. Thus an effort to require work by recipients is worthwhile if it establishes throughout society the essential notion that an individual's benefits are conditioned on the meeting of social obligations, even if the actual numbers brought into such programs are at first small and progress is gradual. In this way, the poor will be treated with the same dignity and respect as other citizens.

7. *Cash benefits should be transitional.* Public assistance is intended as a temporary form of aid, providing help until the recipient—a mother recently widowed or divorced, for example—can become self-supporting. For many current recipients that is exactly how welfare operates. But for a large number of others, AFDC has become a long-term support, often leading to habits of dependency that make attaining self-reliance progressively more difficult. Most who have looked at this problem now agree that public assistance should be restored to its original function. Some, though not all, of the necessary steps are clear:

- For women of mature age thrown into temporary poverty by divorce or separation, transitional aid is in line with the purposes of AFDC. Many such women possess the educational resources, skills, and determination to enable them to become independent within a short time. Programs assisting them, accordingly, should not compromise their independence.

- Those, however, who need preliminary training in personal habits and work skills should be required to enroll for a time in work-training programs or, if necessary and appropriate, to complete work for their high-school diploma or equivalent.

- After a specific time limit (such as two years), a recipient of AFDC should be required, as a condition of further assistance, either to find employment or to accept employment in a public job.

8. *Clear and fair sanctions should be imposed on able recipients of benefits who fail to work without good cause (such as a serious physical or mental disability).* The integrity of AFDC as a transitional program must be upheld. No proposal to reform welfare is worth considering seriously unless it establishes clear sanctions for noncompliance.

Sanctions are important both as signals of the basic values of a free society and as guides to self-development. A welfare policy without clear incentives and sanctions promotes disorientation about values and thus does injustice to those it would help. Sanctions may be constructed positively or negatively, either offering incentives in the form of rewards or denying benefits unless obligations are met. The underlying principle is that the welfare system must be infused with a sense of obligation in order to build a sense of reciprocal bonds among the members of the civic community. That community best helps the able needy by including them within its own productive activities. Such a principle underlies both obligation and sanction.

Accordingly, care must be taken not to allow welfare programs to be governed by a misdirected compassion, in which benefits are offered without reciprocity. That would undermine the humanity of able recipients and would treat them with lesser dignity than other citizens.[3]

All welfare programs need sanctions that prevent flagrant abuses and, more important, signal the path for productive behavior. Such programs have a teaching function. Clear sanctions can warn recipients against dependency or change its nature. Some states have reported that the mere fact of insisting on work has brought significant reductions in the number of applications for benefits; this suggests that some adults were in fact able to care for themselves without depending on the public purse. Others, obliged to work, have reported greater satisfaction in working than in their earlier passivity.

Insistence on clear sanctions, however, is bound to present hard cases that test the seriousness and the wisdom of administrators. There will be cases, for example, in which cutting off the benefits of a parent or parents who do not fulfill their obligations will result in "punishing" the children. Such cases are undeniably difficult. But three considerations must be kept in mind in resolving them: (1) to keep children at risk by allowing their parent or parents to act irresponsibly may be to harm the children even more grievously; (2) to make flagrant exceptions is to undermine the system as a whole; (3) to allow parents to use their children as hostages is to invite massive abuse, while confirming the parents in the hypocrisy of their ways.

Some in the Working Seminar support the termination of all assistance in those cases; most of the others would leave assistance to the children intact while terminating or cutting back assistance to the mother. The lesser sanction, called for under current policy, raises fewer questions about the welfare of the children. For now it is probably sufficient to ensure that this penalty is well enforced, as at present it often is not.

Welfare workers meet many tests of their own wisdom daily and will be greatly helped if administrative regulations and community support strengthen their hand in infusing the most needy and desolate with a sense of public and personal obligation, corresponding to the obligations they fulfill to those they try to help. The dignity and future development of dependent persons can be fulfilled only through a pattern of mutual civic obligations. How could it possibly help recipients to reward them for irresponsibility? Consistency concerning obligations is the best compassion, both for individuals and as a universal signal.

Naturally, since the administration of incentives and sanctions is subject to the counterstrategies of recipients, it almost always involves unintended consequences and unanticipated patterns of behavior. That is why experimentation is needed, in different circumstances and among diverse populations of the needy, to discern what works best in reducing behavioral dependency. The skills and habits of self-reliance are not easily learned, as Tocqueville noted, and only the wisest of administrative methods are likely to be successful. Considerable emphasis must therefore be placed on which programs work and why they work.

In administering sanctions, some have suggested the need for sophisticated "case management" systems, run by professional social workers; others have proposed a system of "contracts" between recipients and welfare agencies, specifying mutual responsibilities periodically renegotiated; still others have argued that existing arrangements can be adapted to meet the demands of more extensive work and training efforts. The experiments now under way in many states, counties, and cities should provide valuable information about the most successful approaches.

Regardless of the particulars, we believe that one general change will have to occur if work requirements are to function successfully: The vast array of rules and procedures that have grown up around access to public assistance programs—frequently as the result of judicial action—must be critically reexamined. Some rulings seek one-sidedly to protect the rights of recipients to benefits, without giving due emphasis to the obligations that recipients have to the rest of society, including the duty to seek to become self-reliant.

The American people want to help all the needy who are unable to care for themselves. They want the able needy to have the same sense of dignity and self-reliance as they themselves have. An insistence on public obligation through a strict work requirement as a condition for the receipt of benefits is consistent both with the work ethic other citizens feel bound to and with the nation's understanding of freedom and responsibility.

9. *The working poor should not be taxed into poverty.* Few groups among the poor are more likely to command public sympathy than those in whose household one or more persons work full time while the family remains below the poverty line. Low wages, a large family, or other conditions may prevent such persons from earning an adequate income despite their best efforts. In the recent past many advocated "cashing out" in-kind benefits and giving such persons cash directly, on the basis of a test of need, to bring their incomes above the poverty line.

What is striking about the current discussion of welfare reform is how little serious support this idea now retains. This turnabout reflects the findings of experiments during the past decade, which revealed that supplementing the incomes of the working poor tended to erode precisely those efforts at self-reliance that many wanted to reinforce. In addition, the practical problems of designing a system of assistance that would provide adequate aid and still preserve incentives to work have proved insurmountable. Above all, such programs seem to undercut the dignity that comes from work, exposing some who do work to ridicule. For some, independence is hard to maintain; the pride that sustains them should not be undermined. Nevertheless, constructive steps can be taken:

116

• At a minimum, taxes should not drive low-income workers below the poverty line. By raising exemptions and the standard deduction, the tax bill of 1986 has essentially lifted the burden of the federal income tax from the working poor. State and local income taxes should be adjusted similarly.

• The working poor remain liable for payroll taxes for social security, which the earned income tax credit (EITC) only partially offsets. Thus some in the Working Seminar favor raising the levels of EITC. Others strongly oppose this, predicting that it would spread some of the dependency-inducing characteristics of current cash-assistance welfare programs to a broader range of citizens. Hence EITC should not be expanded without a detailed calculation of its costs and probable behavioral consequences.

• The Working Seminar did not undertake a study of health care. Yet our concern about dependency led us to note a central problem: on the one hand, about 15 percent of the population, among whom are many who have worked their way out of poverty, lack medical coverage; on the other hand, there is evidence that some persons now stay on welfare primarily to keep Medicaid coverage.[4] Major programmatic experiments are now under way, and a sustained investigation of their results will shortly be in order.

• Finally, although it is self-evident, it seems worth repeating that government most fundamentally helps the working poor by pursuing policies that foster economic growth, deal with labor market inefficiencies, improve education and job-related training, and lead to rising real incomes.

10. *In the administration of welfare, the principle of federalism should be maintained, but policies should be adjusted to emphasize state and local innovation.* In trying to determine which level of government—federal, state, or local—should be in charge of administering and financing public assistance programs, much fruitless argument has often deflected attention from the actual condition of the dependent. Following the model of social security, some have argued that welfare should be entirely paid for and run by Washington. Others have urged total local control. Still others want more federal financing ("fiscal relief") but less federal involvement in administration. As with many disputes over the arrangements of American federalism, no perfect and decisive resolution is ever in sight. Nor should it be, since the vital balance should be allowed to shift from time to time as experience dictates.

The Working Seminar has observed that, with some exceptions, the current consensus has largely bypassed this earlier controversy. From those who have already made their views known (among whom are several governors and an association of state officials), one hears fewer cries for fiscal relief or complaints about federal intrusiveness. By the same token, the White House has pledged continuing federal fiscal support while encouraging the current wave of local experimentation. On all sides the new consensus seems to uphold the principle of federalism. This is generally to the good, since it will enable public discussion to concentrate primarily on the central question—the needs of the poor and the dependent and their corresponding obligations—rather than the mechanism of delivery.

Certain administrative and financial matters do deserve attention, however. Under the current arrangements the federal government, on the one hand, bears a major share of the responsibility for financing public assistance programs. On the other hand, the states and localities are chiefly in charge of delivering services, because of their greater flexibility and closer proximity to those needing help.

The Working Seminar believes that state and local governments should be given great latitude to experiment with methods of reducing poverty and dependency. This motivates states, counties, and local jurisdictions—each in a different way—to find the programs that work best for them. Often the mixture of programs and their coordination are as significant as their individual design. As long as the federal government and the states share costs, the states have a strong incentive to seek their own most effective combination of programs.

This also means that the federal government should review its own rules and regulations, to be sure that they do not unnecessarily complicate or limit state and local initiatives in welfare reform. Thousands of such rules and regulations have grown up around income support programs such as food stamps and public housing, as well as around more general issues such as due process. Some derive from the courts, not from Congress. In the light of the new consensus on welfare, nearly all these rules and regulations need to be reexamined. To deal with behavioral dependency, obligations should be specified as far as possible in law. But a certain amount of discretion is necessary in dealing with individual cases, which excessive regulation may prevent.

A frequent criticism of American public assistance policy has been that benefits are not uniform across the country, even though the current package of assistance (including in-kind benefits such as food stamps) has created a de facto floor, held down by only a few very low-benefit states. Some members of the Working Seminar would like to have this floor standardized across the country, possibly

118

at about two-thirds of the poverty line. We have seen, however, that the poor in the United States are extremely diverse. Neither their behaviors nor their circumstances are uniform. Thus others in our group hold that a standard benefit level would be inconsistent with a social policy that aims to meet individual needs without creating dependency. They fear that raising the floor would expand dependency, diminish the flexibility of the states, and give precisely the wrong moral signal.

In any case, all of us support what we (and others) believe is an underlying principle: that standards for aid to the poor should reflect local living conditions and diverse circumstances since, to cite again an obvious example, the nature of poverty is different in rural Iowa and in inner-city Chicago and since labor market conditions vary widely in various localities.

Notes

1. William J. Bennett, "Address before the 1987 Texas Education Conference," San Antonio, Texas, January 16, 1987.
2. Among the members of the Working Seminar, Richard Nathan has been following experiments in various states and localities most closely. See, e.g., the Manpower Demonstration Research Corporation's "Work Initiatives for Welfare Recipients: Lessons from a Multi-State Experment," March 1986.
3. Mickey Kaus has written in the *New Republic:* "Compassion . . . is a miserable basis for liberal politics. It carries the unmistakable implication of dependence and piteousness on the part of those on the receiving end of the sentiment. . . . *Compassion* . . . provides no principle to tell us when our abstract compassionate impulses should stop. . . . Compassion makes few distinctions." "Up from Altruism," *New Republic,* December 15, 1986 (emphasis in original).
4. According to the Census Bureau's "Survey of Income and Program Participation," 13.3 percent of the U.S. population had no health insurance coverage in the fourth quarter of 1985; 12.4 percent of whites were uncovered, 19.3 percent of blacks, 27.0 percent of Hispanics. Of those persons who were covered, 88 percent relied on private health insurance. See Robert D. Reischauer, "Welfare Reform and the Working Poor" (Paper prepared for inclusion in *Reducing Poverty and Dependency,* forthcoming in 1987 from the Center for National Policy), p. 29, mimeo. The noncovered poor are more likely to be found among the near poor and working poor than among the fully dependent population. For instance, in the year 1984, an AFDC mother with two children had an average of $1,700 spent on her family by the government for Medicaid coverage. See Committee on Ways and Means, U.S. House of Representatives, *Background Material and Data on Programs within the Jurisdiction of the Committee on Ways and Means* (Washington, D.C.: U.S. Government Printing Office, 1986), p. 255, table 3.

119

8

Conclusion

Judging from the recent outpouring of interest in welfare policy, the United States stands poised on the brink of a new era of social inventiveness, a challenging period in which to imagine new ways to do things. Government itself can do more and do it better if its leaders and administrators employ the inventiveness that has characterized all creative eras of American life. But through, around, over, and under government, all the people and all their associations need to cooperate more closely and work more imaginatively if we are really to help the poor.

What does it mean, "to help the poor"? Some are elderly, disabled, or otherwise in need of income support. Many of these also need personal services.[1] Others—the young and able poor—need income supports less than they need instruction in the skills, habits, and attitudes through which to achieve independence and to make the productive contributions society needs from them.

Income support has its difficulties but is, by comparison, relatively straightforward. But helping the poor is not merely a matter of distributing money. Behavioral dependency and the dysfunctions associated with it require the attention of the whole society.

Dependency will not go away through economic growth alone or through government action alone. In many places it has evidently become encysted and is now impenetrable except by the concerted efforts of all, in a more intensive and imaginative way than the nation foresaw two decades ago.

To be sure, there will never be a time when there are no poor persons in need of special help, services, or income supports. Human nature and life's vicissitudes will see to that. The nation's goal, therefore, should be not to "eliminate" poverty but to reduce it as much as possible by adapting quickly to its ever new forms and unforeseen necessities. The problems associated with the underclass, as we have seen, today require a new agenda.

No person should be involuntarily poor without having assistance available from others. No able adult should be allowed voluntarily to take from the common good without also contributing to it. Low income and behavioral dependency are two quite different problems and should be met by different remedies.

A free society sets unusually high expectations for its able citizens. It demands the self-reliance of each, so that each may contribute productively to the well-being of all. The United States is a community of a special sort, made up of free, self-determining persons: a community of self-reliance, in which independence is made possible by mutual cooperation and in which community is aimed at self-development.

Concerning both poverty and behavioral dependency, the entire nation can do better. The reports of the past few months show that many now agree on the basic principles for doing better. What we need is to put these principles into concrete practice, at every appropriate level and in every locality. The children of the needy, especially, depend on us.

Note

1. According to a General Accounting Office study using the government's 1982 long-term care survey, 1.1 million elderly said they had some help with basic activities but needed more. Another 168,000 lacked regular help with one or more fundamental activities. Of those 1.9 million who said all their needs were being met, 71 percent said their relatives provided unpaid help. Another 21 percent said their care came from both paid and unpaid help. Very few relied entirely on paid care. See Spencer Rich, "Daily Needs Not Met for Many Elderly," *Washington Post*, January 17, 1987.

Appendix

The following tables contain data pertaining to the nature of poverty, the condition of the family, and the state of social programs in the United States today and in the recent past. In the interests of readability, the use of statistics was kept to a minimum in the body of the report. These additional tables may be of use to the specialist but also to the general reader interested in investigating further some of the evidence that has come to shape the impressions of the Working Seminar.

Tables 1 through 4 present data pertaining to poverty and affluence. The poverty rate for subgroups in the United States differs dramatically with age, race, and family structure. Earnings are also closely associated with differences in educational attainment. Poverty rates as officially constructed measure only current money income—not public benefits in kind or household net worth. For these and other reasons, the difference between a household's money income and the amount it can actually spend may be quite substantial; expenditures of households in the lower levels of income distribution, taken in total, appear to exceed pretax income by a considerable margin.

Tables 5 through 12 present data pertaining to some of the government-funded programs that have been fashioned to help forestall poverty or to alleviate its consequences. Between 1940 and 1960, the fraction of national resources spent on public assistance and public aid declined; between 1960 and 1980, it rose rapidly. Means-tested benefits—those awarded to those defined as needy—have increasingly been transfers in kind, rather than cash grants. Participation in public benefit programs differs widely by age, race, and family structure. The Aid for Families with Dependent Children program (AFDC) is perhaps the best known of the public assistance programs. About three-fifths of the children receiving benefits from this program live in ten states. The nature of the AFDC program has changed dramatically since its inception: originally a benefit program primarily for children with dead or incapacitated fathers, the program today provides the largest share of its benefits to children born of unwed mothers. The fraction of illegitimate children in the nation who are on the AFDC program appears to have risen steadily over the life of the program.

Tables 13, 14, and 15 pertain to illegitimacy and family structure. The fraction of children born to mothers who reported themselves to be unwed has risen steadily for every age group and all races since 1940. An increasing percentage of children live in female-headed households, even though increasing longevity has meant that a smaller fraction of women and children are widowed and orphaned today than ever before.

Tables 16 through 19 pertain to health status. After a slowdown in the 1950s and 1960s, improvements in life expectancy accelerated in the 1970s and the early 1980s. A gap in health levels exists between white and black Americans, but the gap in life expectancy has been narrowed during the recent period of more rapid improvements. Infant mortality is another important indicator of popular health. Interestingly, there has been no correspondence between trends in infant mortality and trends in the official poverty rate since the early 1970s; for the period 1973 to 1983, in fact, the trends of these two indicators pointed in opposite directions. Family status, and particularly legitimacy status, may be a better predictor of infant mortality than poverty as it is officially measured.

Tables 20 and 21 pertain to food. American consumers have tended to devote a decreasing proportion of their total expenditures to food over the past century; this trend seems to have continued over the most recent decades as well. By one attempt to reach an estimate, Americans eligible to receive food stamps devoted less of their personal consumption expenditures to food than did the general populations of many Western nations.

Tables 22 and 23 pertain to subgroups in the U.S. population that remain difficult to enumerate. Neither social programs nor private charities can be fully efficacious in assisting persons who are, in some sense, socially invisible. Although the overall level of estimated undercounting in the U.S. decennial censuses has been progressively reduced, significant differences remain according to race. The fraction of households without telephones has similarly declined; differentials between groups remain pronounced, according to both race and age.

TABLE A-1

PORTRAIT OF OFFICIAL POVERTY, 1985

	Below Poverty Level (thousands)	Poverty Rate (percent)
All persons	33,064	14.0
White	22,860	11.4
Black	8,926	31.3
Hispanic[a]	5,236	29.0
Under 15 years of age	11,110	21.5
15–24 years	6,363	16.6
25–44 years	7,899	10.6
45–54 years	1,911	8.4
55–59 years	1,103	9.8
60–64 years	1,222	11.3
65 years and over	3,456	12.6
Northeast	5,751	11.6
Midwest	8,191	13.9
South	12,921	16.0
West	6,201	13.0
All related children under 18 years of age	12,814	20.5
White	8,082	15.9
Black	4,136	43.4
Hispanic[a]	2,558	39.9
In families	12,483	20.1
In unrelated subfamilies	331	54.1
All families	7,223	11.4
White	4,983	9.1
Black	1,983	28.7
Hispanic[a]	1,074	25.5
Married-couple families	3,438	6.7
Female householder, no husband present	3,474	34.0
Male householder, no wife present	311	12.9
All unrelated individuals	6,725	21.5
Male	2,499	17.4
Female	4,226	24.8

a. Persons of Hispanic origin may be of any race.

SOURCE: U.S. Bureau of the Census, *Money Income and Poverty Status of Families and Persons in the United States: 1985*, table A.

TABLE A–2

AVERAGE FAMILY INCOME
BY EDUCATION OF HOUSEHOLD HEAD, 1983
(dollars)

Education	Average Family Income
0–8 grades	7,706
9–11 grades	10,975
High school diploma	15,390
Some college	17,739
Bachelor's degree	28,764

SOURCE: John Weicher and Susan Wachter, "The Distribution of Wealth among Families" (Paper presented to the Working Seminar on the Family and American Welfare Policy).

TABLE A–3

FAMILY NET WORTH, 1983
(dollars)

Characteristic of Family Head	Average Net Worth
Age	
17–24	4,531
25–34	16,651
35-44	40,710
45–54	56,320
55–64	82,115
65–74	84,499
75+	48,749
Marital status	
Married couple	
With children	39,569
Without children	78,567
Female-headed family	
With children	14,967
Without children	38,237
Education	
0–8 years	22,351
9–11 years	28,053
High school diploma	37,680
Some college	54,278
Bachelor's degree	82,770

TABLE A–3 (continued)

Characteristic of Family Head	Average Net Worth
Race	
White	52,820
Black	16,766
Hispanic[a]	15,318

NOTE: Net worth is defined as financial assets plus equity in a home plus equity in other real estate (specifically farms and apartments). The value of pensions, social security credits, unincorporated businesses, household durable goods, cars, boats, and some other items is not included.

a. Persons of Hispanic origin may be of any race.

SOURCE: John Weicher and Susan Wachter, "The Distribution of Wealth among Families" (Paper presented to the Working Seminar on the Family and American Welfare Policy), tables 2–5.

TABLE A–4

TOTAL INCOME BEFORE TAXES AND PERSONAL CONSUMPTION
EXPENDITURES FOR URBAN HOUSEHOLDS,
BY INCOME QUINTILE, 1982–1983
(dollars)

	Lowest 20 Percent	Second 20 Percent	Third 20 Percent	Fourth 20 Percent	Highest 20 Percent	All Complete Reporting Households
Income before taxes	4,097	10,611	18,129	28,231	52,267	22,702
Total expenditures	8,324	12,155	16,733	22,425	35,171	18,981
Expenditures as percentage of income before taxes	203	115	92	79	67	84

SOURCE: U.S. Bureau of the Census, *Statistical Abstract of the United States, 1986.*

TABLE A–5
PUBLIC ASSISTANCE, "PUBLIC AID," SOCIAL INSURANCE, AND PERSONAL SAVINGS AS A PERCENTAGE OF PERSONAL INCOME, 1929–1983

	Public Assistance Programs[a] (1)	"Public Aid"[b] (2)	"Social Insurance"[c] (3)	Personal Savings Rate[d] (4)
1929	0.1	0.1	0.4	3.9
1940	3.4	4.2	1.6	4.3
1950	1.0	1.1 (1.3)	2.2	5.3
1955	0.8	1.0	3.2	5.4
1960	0.8	1.0 (1.0)	4.8	4.9
1965	0.8	1.2 (1.6)	5.2	6.4
1970	1.2	2.0 (2.6)	6.8	7.4
1973	1.3	3.0 (3.7)	9.4	7.8
1975	1.7	3.3 (4.1)	9.8	7.4
1980	1.4	3.3 (4.4)	10.6	6.0
1983	1.3	3.1 (3.9)	12.0	4.3

a. Includes AFDC, general assistance, aid to the blind, old age assistance, and aid to the permanently and totally disabled.

b. Includes all programs in column (1), work relief, general emergency aid, food stamps, surplus food for the needy, repatriate and refugee assistance, work experience, training programs, and Low Income Home Energy Assistance. Parenthetical total includes housing and "other social welfare," as categorized by the *Social Security Bulletin*.

c. Includes OASDHI, Medicare, railroad retirement, public employee retirement, unemployment insurance and employment service, railroad unemployment insurance, railroad temporary disability insurance, and workers' compensation.

d. Personal savings in relation to disposable personal income.

SOURCE: U.S. Social Security Administration, *Social Security Bulletin Annual Statistical Supplement.*

128

TABLE A–6

GOVERNMENT EXPENDITURES FOR MEANS-TESTED ASSISTANCE,
1970–1983
(thousands of 1984 dollars)

	1970	1975	1979	1980	1981	1982	1983
Means-tested cash assistance[a]	19,070	34,546	33,130	32,137	30,710	29,276	28,875
Means-tested noncash benefits[b]	21,195	38,164	47,152	49,253	51,768	50,486	51,988
Total	40,265	72,710	80,282	81,390	82,478	79,762	80,863
Noncash as percentage of total	52.6	52.5	58.7	60.5	62.8	63.3	64.3

a. Includes AFDC, general assistance, SSI, and means-tested veterans' pensions.
b. Includes food stamps, free and reduced-price school lunches, public and subsidized housing, and Medicaid; excludes domestic agricultural commodity disposal.
SOURCE: Derived from U.S. Bureau of the Census, *Estimates of Poverty Including the Value of Noncash Benefits: 1984*, Technical Paper 55.

TABLE A–7

CENSUS BUREAU CPS ESTIMATES OF PARTICIPATION RATES FOR
SELECTED CATEGORIES OF HOUSEHOLDS IN SELECTED PUBLIC
BENEFIT PROGRAMS, 1983
(percentage of households)

Household Category	Public Assistance	Supplemental Security Income	Social Security
All families	5.7	2.6	22.9
White families	3.7	2.0	23.2
Black families	20.9	7.4	22.0
White families below poverty line	27.4	5.8	17.7
Black families below poverty line	52.4	12.1	21.5
Female householder families	23.9	6.5	27.5
Male householder families	2.3	1.8	22.0

(table continues)

129

TABLE A–7 (continued)

Household Category	Public Assistance	Supplemental Security Income	Social Security
All families with householders under 25	17.5	0.8	1.7
All families with householders 25–64	5.7	2.0	10.4
All families with householders 65+	1.4	6.5	93.6
Unrelated individuals	1.9	4.7	31.7

SOURCE: U.S. Bureau of the Census, *Characteristics of the Population below the Poverty Level: 1983.*

TABLE A–8

HOUSEHOLDS IN WHICH ONE OR MORE PERSONS RECEIVED GOVERNMENT-PROVIDED, MEANS-TESTED NONCASH BENEFITS, FOURTH QUARTER, 1984
(percent)

	One or More Programs	Food Stamps
All households	17.0	7.2
Households with no members with labor force activity	28.8	15.4
Households with one or more members looking for work or on layoff	36.2	20.2
Households with one or more members with a job or business, no member looking for work or on layoff	10.2	2.5
Type of households		
Family householder	17.6	7.6
Female householder, no husband present, with own children under 18 years	59.8	38.5

130

TABLE A–8 (continued)

	One or More Programs	Food Stamps
Nonfamily households		
Male householder	10.2	4.0
Female householder	19.5	7.9
Age of householder		
15–24 years	18.4	11.1
25–34 years	18.9	8.8
35–44 years	16.3	6.6
45–54 years	15.2	6.0
55–64 years	13.4	5.6
65 years +	19.4	6.7
Work disability of householder		
Householder, 16 to 64 years of age	16.5	7.3
With work disability	33.8	18.3
With retirement or disability income	36.6	16.9
With no work disability	13.7	5.5
Place of residence		
Outside metropolitan areas	19.9	9.1
Inside metropolitan areas	16.2	6.6
Under 1 million people	16.0	6.6
1 million people or more	16.3	6.6
Race		
White	13.4	5.1
Black	43.6	22.7
Hispanic origin[a]	38.2	15.7

NOTE: Programs include food stamps, WIC, free or reduced-priced school meals, public or subsidized rental housing, and Medicaid or Medicare.

a. Persons of Hispanic origin may be of any race.

SOURCE: U.S. Bureau of the Census, *Economic Characteristics of Households in the United States: Fourth Quarter 1984*.

TABLE A–9

HOUSEHOLDS RECEIVING GOVERNMENT-PROVIDED, MEANS-TESTED
CASH BENEFITS WHO DID NOT ALSO RECEIVE GOVERNMENT-PROVIDED,
MEANS-TESTED NONCASH BENEFITS, FOURTH QUARTER, 1984
(percent)

All households	12.0
Households with no members with labor force activity	9.0
Households with one or more members looking for work	3.0
Households with one or more members with a job or business, no member looking for work	18.2
Family households	
All family	10.7
Married-couple families	20.5
Female householder, no husband present, with own children under 18 years of age	1.5
Nonfamily households	
Male householder	14.3
Female householder	10.9
Age of householder	
15–24 years	1.0
25–34 years	2.7
35–44 years	4.8
45–54 years	8.5
55–64 years	22.7
65 years and over	18.4
Residence of households	
Outside metropolitan areas	25.3
Inside metropolitan area	9.9
Under 1 million people	15.1
1 million people or more	8.1
Race of households	
White	15.4
Black	3.9
Hispanic[a]	2.3

a. Persons of Hispanic origin may be of any race.
SOURCE: Derived from U.S. Bureau of the Census, *Economic Characteristics of Households in the United States: Fourth Quarter 1984.*

TABLE A-10

TEN LARGEST AFDC POPULATIONS, BY STATE, 1984
(numbers in thousands)

	Families		Recipients	
State	Number	Percentage of U.S. total	Total	Children
California	548	15	1,603	1,058
New York	372	10	1,112	731
Illinois	240	6	733	491
Michigan	227	6	696	444
Ohio	224	6	670	422
Pennsylvania	187	5	558	368
New Jersey	125	3	368	247
Texas	117	3	351	247
Florida	98	3	271	190
Wisconsin	93	3	280	176
Top ten states combined	2,231	60	6,642	4,374
All states	3,700	100	10,800	7,100

SOURCE: U.S. Social Security Administration, *Social Security Bulletin*, September 1986, table M-29.

TABLE A-11

CHARACTERISTICS OF FATHERS OF CHILDREN RECEIVING AFDC BENEFITS, 1937–1982
(percent)

Year	Father Deceased	Father Incapacitated	Father Not Married to Mother
1937–38	48.4	22.8	2.8
1940–41	22.7	34.2	3.1
1948[a]	22.8	22.6	14.1
1961	6.9	21.4	18.2
1967	5.5	12.0	26.8
1975	3.7	7.7	31.0
1982	0.9	3.5	46.5

a. Data for 1948 refers to total AFDC families, not AFDC children.

SOURCES: Bureau of Public Assistance, "Changes in the Types of Families Accepted for Aid to Dependent Children," *Social Security Bulletin*, June 1943; Elizabeth Alling and

(continued)

133

Agnes Leisy, "Aid to Dependent Children in a Postwar Year," *Social Security Bulletin,* August 1950; Robert M. Mugge, "Aid to Families with Dependent Children: Initial Findings of the 1961 Report on Characteristics of Recipients," *Social Security Bulletin,* March 1963; National Center for Social Statistics, "Findings of the 1967 AFDC Study: Data by State Aid Census Division"; and Bureau of the Census, *Statistical Abstract of the United States 1986.*

TABLE A–12

CHARACTERISTICS OF AFDC CHILDREN
OF UNWED MOTHERS, 1940–1982

Year	Total Number (thousands)	As a Percentage of All Children under 18	As a Percentage of All Children in Female-headed Households Whose Head Has Never Married	As a Percentage of Children in Female-headed Families, Including Those Headed by Divorcees and Widows
1940[a]	28	0.07	5[b,c]	3[b,c]
1961[d]	432	0.6	85[b]	22[b]
1967	1,068	1.5	232[c]	44[b]
1975	2,513	3.8	234	53
1982	3,242	5.2	151	59

a. AFDC characteristics for 1940–1941, U.S. household and population characteristics for 1940 (April).

b. Calculations use "related children under 18" rather than "all children under 18" and allocates children in female householder families proportionately to marital status category listed for female householders.

c. Computation assumes that the average number of children in female householder families with three or more children was 4.0 and allocates children among female-headed households, rather than families, proportionately by listed marital status.

d. AFDC characteristics for 1960–1961; U.S. household and population characteristics for 1961.

SOURCES: Derived from Nicholas Eberstadt, "Economic and Material Poverty in America" (Paper presented to the Working Seminar on the Family and Welfare Reform, table 31); *Social Security Bulletin,* various issues; Bureau of the Census, *Household and Family Characteristics: March 1982; idem, Household and Family Characteristics: March 1975.*

TABLE A–13

NUMBER AND CHARACTERISTICS OF ESTIMATED ILLEGITIMATE BIRTHS, 1940–1983

	Total Number	White	Nonwhite	Black	All Races	White	Nonwhite (% of births)	Black
1940	89,500	40,300	49,200	n.a.	3.8	2.0	16.8	n.a.
1950	141,600	53,500	88,100	n.a.	4.0	1.8	18.0	n.a.
1959	220,600	79,600	141,100	n.a.	5.2	2.2	21.8	n.a.
1960	224,300	82,000	141,800	n.a.	5.3	2.3	21.6	n.a.
1970	398,700	175,000	223,600	215,000	10.7	5.7	34.9	37.6
1973	407,300	163,800	237,500	229,000	13.0	6.4	41.7	45.8
1980	665,747	320,063	345,684	325,737	18.4	11.0	48.5	55.3
1983	737,893	370,884	367,009	341,077	20.3	12.8	50.0	58.2

n.a. = not available.

SOURCES: "Advance Report of Final Natality Statistics, 1983," *Monthly Vital Statistics Report*, vol. 34, no. 6, Supplement, September 20, 1985; National Center for Health Statistics, *Vital Statistics United States: Volume I, Natality*, various issues; National Office of Vital Statistics, *Vital Statistics of the United States, 1950: Volume I, Natality*; U.S. Bureau of the Census, *Fertility Indicators: 1970*; and U.S. Bureau of the Census, *Statistical Abstract of the United States, 1971*.

TABLE A–14

DISTRIBUTION OF ESTIMATED ILLEGITIMATE BIRTHS BY AGE OF MOTHER, 1940–1983

	15–19	20–24	25–29	30–34	35–39	40 +
As a Percentage of All Estimated Illegitimate Births						
1940, All races	45.2	30.4	11.2	5.8	3.4	1.1
1950, All races	39.5	30.4	14.8	7.6	4.2	1.2
White	37.2	33.3	14.8	7.9	4.3	1.3
Nonwhite	41.0	28.7	14.8	7.5	4.1	1.1
1960, All races	38.8	30.3	14.3	8.4	4.7	1.3
White	39.8	32.3	13.0	7.3	4.7	1.6
Nonwhite	38.3	29.1	15.0	9.1	4.7	1.2
1970, All races	71.7	31.8	10.2	4.8	2.4	0.8
White	45.3	35.5	10.3	4.4	2.3	0.8
Nonwhite	79.7	28.9	10.1	5.0	2.4	0.8
Black	79.0	28.7	9.9	5.0	2.4	0.7

(table continues)

135

TABLE A–14 (continued)

1973, All races	50.3	24.2	10.6	4.5	2.0	0.6
White	49.8	29.6	11.2	4.7	2.1	0.7
Nonwhite	50.7	69.0	10.1	4.5	2.0	0.6
Black	51.1	28.8	10.0	4.4	2.0	0.6
1980, All races	39.5	35.6	15.0	6.2	2.0	0.4
White	40.0	35.3	14.6	6.4	2.2	0.5
Nonwhite	39.0	36.0	15.2	5.9	1.8	0.4
Black	39.3	36.0	15.0	5.8	1.7	0.4
1983, All races	35.4	36.0	17.1	7.3	2.5	0.5
White	35.7	35.7	16.8	7.5	2.8	0.6
Nonwhite	35.1	36.3	17.5	7.1	2.1	0.4
Black	35.5	36.3	17.3	6.9	2.1	0.4
As a Percentage of All Births in Cohort						
1940–44, All races	13.5	3.5	1.5	1.3	1.5	1.6
1950, All races	13.3	3.8	2.0	1.8	2.0	2.1
White	6.2	2.0	0.9	0.8	0.9	1.0
Nonwhite	35.8	15.9	11.5	10.2	9.9	9.3
1960, All races	14.8	4.8	2.9	2.8	3.0	3.1
White	7.2	2.2	1.1	1.0	1.3	1.6
Nonwhite	42.1	20.0	14.1	12.9	12.8	11.7
1970, All races	29.5	8.9	4.1	4.5	5.2	5.7
White	17.1	5.2	2.0	2.1	2.7	3.3
Nonwhite	61.4	29.5	12.1	17.3	16.9	16.9
Black	62.7	31.3	20.3	19.6	18.6	10.3
1973, All races	33.4	10.8	4.9	5.0	6.5	7.7
White	19.1	5.3	2.4	2.4	3.3	4.1
Nonwhite	69.1	35.9	21.8	19.4	20.2	20.0
Black	71.0	38.6	25.7	23.3	22.9	23.2
1980, All races	47.6	19.4	9.0	7.5	9.4	12.1
White	33.0	11.5	5.0	4.5	6.3	8.5
Nonwhite	82.1	51.1	30.1	22.4	22.1	23.6
Black	85.2	56.0	36.2	29.2	28.1	29.3
1983, All races	53.4	22.9	11.0	8.6	10.9	13.4
White	39.2	14.4	6.5	8.4	7.0	10.0
Nonwhite	85.2	54.9	33.5	25.0	23.1	25.1
Black	88.5	61.0	41.1	33.1	31.3	32.2

SOURCES: "Advance Report of Final Natality Statistics, 1983," *Monthly Vital Statistics Report*, vol. 34, no. 6, Supplement September 20, 1985; National Center for Health Statistics, *Vital Statistics United States: Volume I, Natality*, various issues; National Office of Vital Statistics, *Vital Statistics of the United States, 1950: Volume I, Natality*; U.S. Bureau of the Census, *Fertility Indicators: 1970*; and U.S. Bureau of the Census, *Statistical Abstract of the United States, 1971*.

TABLE A–15

CHARACTERISTICS OF FEMALE-HEADED HOUSEHOLDS WITH CHILDREN
UNDER EIGHTEEN YEARS OF AGE, BY RACE AND MARITAL STATUS,
1959, 1973, AND 1983

	1959[a]	1973	1983
Householder, all races			
Widowed	51.7	24.4	14.1
Divorced	15.4	32.8	42.5
Married, husband absent	24.5	36.6	23.3
Single, never married	8.4	10.6	19.6
Householder white			
Widowed	52.5	25.7	14.1
Divorced	18.1	42.0	53.2
Married, husband absent	17.8	27.3	23.3
Single, never married	11.8	5.0	10.6
Householder black			
Widowed	40.2[b]	21.9	13.9
Divorced	11.6[b]	16.8	24.0
Married, husband absent	37.4[b]	40.1	25.4
Single, never married	10.8[b]	21.2	36.6

*Children under 18 in Female-headed Families,
as a Percentage of All Children under 18*

All persons	9.1	14.2	19.4
White	5.6	9.7	14.0
Black	27.2[b]	40.9	49.6
Hispanic[c]	n.a.	n.a.	25.0

*Children under 18 in Families Headed by Widows,
as a Percentage of All Children in Female-Headed Families*

All races	42.5	22.8	13.3
White	44.7	23.2	12.9
Black	35.8[b]	21.9	13.2
Hispanic[c]	n.a.	n.a.	10.5

(table continues)

TABLE A–15 (continued)

	1959[a]	1973	1983

Children under 18 in Families Headed by Widows,
as a Percentage of All Children under 18

All races	3.8	3.2	2.6
White	2.5	2.2	1.8
Black	9.7[b]	9.0	6.5
Hispanic[c]	n.a.	n.a.	2.7

n.a. = not available.

a. Calculations as for all female-headed families, including those *without* children under 18 years of age. For whites and "nonwhites," data are for 1960.

b. "Nonwhites" includes other groups besides black and Hispanic.

c. "Hispanic" may be of any race.

SOURCES: Derived from U.S. Bureau of the Census, *Household and Family Characteristics: March 1983; idem, Household and Family Characteristics: March 1973; idem, Family Characteristics of Persons: March 1959; idem, Household and Family Characteristics: March 1959; idem, Statistical Abstract of the United Staes*, various issues.

TABLE A–16

LIFE EXPECTANCY AT BIRTH, 1940–1983
(years)

	All Persons	Annual Rate of Change	Whites	Annual Rate of Change	Blacks	Annual Rate of Change
1940	62.9		64.2		53.1	
		0.59		0.49		0.77
1950	68.2		69.1		60.8	
		0.15		0.15		0.28
1960	69.7		70.6		63.6	
		0.11		0.11		0.17
1970	70.8		71.7		65.3	
		0.29		0.27		0.42
1980	73.7		74.4		69.5	
		0.33		0.27		0.67
1983[a]	74.7		75.2		71.3	

a. Preliminary data.

SOURCES: U.S. Bureau of the Census, *Statistical Abstract of the United States,* various issues.

138

TABLE A–17

INFANT MORTALITY RATES, 1940–1983
(per 1,000 live births)

	All Races	Percentage Change	Per Annum Change	Whites	Blacks
1940	47.0			43.2	72.9
		– 37.9	– 4.6		
1950	29.2			26.8	43.9
		– 11.0	– 1.2		
1960	26.0			22.9	44.3
		– 23.1	– 2.6		
1970	20.0			17.8	32.6
		– 37.0	– 4.5		
1980	12.6			11.0	21.8
		– 11.9	– 4.1		
1983	11.1			9.7	19.2

SOURCES: U.S. Bureau of the Census, *Statistical Abstract of the United States 1986*; National Center for Health Statistics, "Advance Report of Final Mortality Statistics, 1983," *Monthly Vital Statistics Report*, Supplement (2), September 26, 1985; *idem, Vital Statistics of the United States*, various issues.

TABLE A–18

INFANT MORTALITY RATES AND ESTIMATED POVERTY RATE FOR RELATED CHILDREN UNDER EIGHTEEN, 1960–1983

	1960	1965	1973	1975	1980	1983
All races						
Infant mortality	26.0	24.7	17.7	16.1	12.6	11.0
Poverty	26.5	16.3	14.2	16.8	17.9	21.7
White						
Infant mortality	22.9	21.5	15.8	14.2	11.0	9.7
Poverty	20.0	14.4	9.7	12.5	13.4	16.9
Nonwhites						
Infant mortality	43.2	40.3	26.2	24.2	19.1	16.8
Poverty	66.6	59.0	38.9	38.0	38.3	42.8
Blacks						
Infant mortality	44.3	41.7	28.1	26.2	21.8	19.2
Poverty	n.a.	47.4[a]	40.7	41.4	42.1	46.3

n.a. = not available.
NOTES: Infant mortality rates per 1,000 live births; poverty rate as percentage of related children under eighteen.
a. 1967.
SOURCE: U.S. Bureau of the Census, Series P-60, various issues; *idem, Statistical Abstract of the United States*, various issues.

TABLE A–19
Infant Mortality Rates and Other Child Risk Indicators for Various Ethnic Groups, 1980

	Infant Mortality Rate per 1,000 live births	Low Birth Weight (percent)	Teen-age Mothers (percent)	Unmarried Mothers (percent)	Poverty Rate for Related Children under 18
All U.S.	12.6	6.8	15.6	18.4	17.9
White	11.0	5.7	13.5	11.0	11.0
Black	21.4	12.5	26.5	55.3	37.8
Hispanic[a]	n.a.	6.9	18.5	24.5	29.1
Mexican	n.a.	5.6	19.4	20.7	n.a.
Puerto Rican	n.a.	9.0	23.1	48.0	n.a.
Chinese	5.3	4.9	1.6	3.3	14.3
Japanese	4.5	6.2	3.8	5.6	5.5
Filipino	5.0	7.4	6.6	9.0	10.1
Other Asian or Pacific Islander	7.9[b]	6.8	5.9	6.1	21.8
Native American, Aleut, and Eskimo[c]	13.2	6.5	23.5	n.a.	32.5

n.a. = Not available.

a. Data for Hispanic population for 1981.

b. Data for population in states served by Indian Health Service.

c. Data on infant mortality includes Hawaiians, who are not included in other figures for the category.

SOURCES: Selma Taffel, "Characteristics of Asian Births, 1980," *Monthly Vital Statistics Report*, vol. 32, no. 10, Supplement, February 10, 1984; Stephanie J. Ventura, "Births of Hispanic Parentage, 1981," *Monthly Vital Statistics Report*, vol. 33, no. 8, Supplement, December 11, 1984; Indian Health Service, *Chart Series Book April 1986*; unpublished data, Indian Health Service; National Center for Health Statistics, *Vital Statistics for the United States, 1980*; and U.S. Bureau of the Census, *1980 Census of Population: chapter C, part 1: General Social and Economic Characteristics*.

TABLE A–20

EXPENDITURES ON FOOD AND NONALCOHOLIC BEVERAGES
AS A PERCENTAGE OF ALL PERSONAL CONSUMPTION EXPENDITURE,
1960/61–1984
(by income quintile)

Household Income Level	1960–61	1972–73	1980–81[a]	1984[a]
Lowest fifth	29.2	22.7	23.2	18.8
Second fifth	26.6	21.9	21.2	17.7
Third fifth	25.2	20.3	19.2	16.4
Fourth fifth	24.7	19.7	18.0	15.1
Highest fifth	22.8	17.9	16.2	13.1
All households with complete reporting	24.5	19.3	18.5	15.6

a. 1980–81 and 1984 data are for urban households.
SOURCES: Bureau of Labor Statistics, *Handbook of Labor Statistics*, various issues; *idem*, "Consumer Expenditure Survey Results from 1984," *News: United States Department of Labor*, June 22, 1986.

TABLE A–21

EXPENDITURES ALLOCATED TO FOOD
AS A PERCENTAGE OF HOUSEHOLD PERSONAL CONSUMPTION
FOR UNITED STATES AND SELECTED OTHER COUNTRIES
(excluding alcoholic beverages)

	Year	Percentage of Total Personal Consumption Spent on Food
United States	1977–78	18.0
Low Income[a]	1977–78	19.1[b]
Israel	1975–76	19.6
Norway	1974–76	22.6
Netherlands	1974–75	23.8
Finland	1976	23.9
Austria	1974	24.5
Belgium[c]	1973–74	25.0
Japan	1979	30.3
Italy	1978	30.5
Singapore	1977–78	48.8

a. "Low income" defined as receiving food stamps or eligible for food stamps.
b. Hybrid estimate derived from 1977–78 USDA Food Consumption Survey and 1982–83 Consumer Expenditure Survey.
c. Data for "workers" only, definition of worker set by criteria of Belgian government.
SOURCES: Food and Agriculture Organization of the United Nations, *Review of Food*

(continued)

141

Consumption Summary 1981; U.S. Department of Agriculture, *Food Consumption, Prices, and Expenditures 1964–84.*

TABLE A–22

ESTIMATED NET UNDERCOUNTING OF U.S. POPULATION
IN CENSUS COUNTS, 1950–1980
(percent)

	1980[a]	1970	1960	1950
All persons	1.0	2.8	3.3	4.4
Male	1.9	3.6	3.8	4.8
Female	[b]	2.0	2.8	4.1
All black persons	5.6	7.9	8.3	9.6
Male	8.5	10.5	10.4	11.7
Female	2.8	5.5	6.2	7.5
All whites and				
other races	0.3	2.1	2.7	3.8
Male	1.0	2.7	3.0	4.0
Female	− 0.3[c]	1.6	2.4	3.6

a. Assumes 2.06 million in undocumented aliens.
b. Under 0.1 percent.
c. Negative sign indicates estimated overcount of population group.
SOURCE: Jeffrey S. Passel and J. Gregory Robinson, "Revised Demographic Estimates of the Coverage of the Population by Age, Sex and Race in the 1980 Census" (Unpublished paper, U.S. Bureau of the Census, April 8, 1985), table 2.

TABLE A–23

PERCENTAGE OF HOUSEHOLDS WITHOUT TELEPHONES,
MARCH 1960 AND NOVEMBER 1983

	1960	1983
All households	22.9	8.6
White	21.5	6.9
Black	44.9[a]	21.2
Householder under age 25	43.9	23.4[b]
Householder aged 25–54	20.5	8.5
Householder aged 55–64	20.0	5.0
Householder aged 65 +	28.0	4.5

a. Data for nonwhites.
b. Householder 16–24 years of age.
SOURCE: U.S. Bureau of the Census, "Characteristics of Households with Telephones, March 1960"; and *idem*, unpublished data.

142

Papers Commissioned for the Working Seminar on the Family and American Welfare Policy

Besharov, Douglas J. "How Child Abuse Programs Hurt Poor Children: The Misuse of Foster Care."

————. "Family Breakdown and Family Poverty: Not All Female-Headed Families Are Created Equal."

Eberstadt, Nick. "Economic and Material Poverty in Modern America."

Hartle, Terry W. and Andrea Bilson. "Increasing the Educational Achievement of Disadvantaged Children: Do Federal Programs Make a Difference?"

Jacobs, Bruce. "The Elderly: How Do They Fare?"

Loury, Glenn C. "Race and Poverty: The Problem of Dependency in a Pluralistic Society."

Mead, Lawrence M. "The Work Problem in Welfare."

Moran, Donald W. "Welfare Dependency: Public Policy versus Public Intentions."

Murray, Charles. "According to Age."

Schiller, Bradley R. "Workfare: An Update."

Starr, Roger. "Neighborhoods and Poverty."

Weicher, John C. and Susan B. Wachter. "The Distribution of Wealth among Families: Increasing Inequality."